SunKissed

An Anthology of Lesbian Love Stories

from

Freya Publications

Visit Freya Publications

At

www.freyapublications.com

Produced in the United Kingdom for Freya Publications

SunKissed
First Published 1st June 2012 by Freya Publications

ISBN – 978-1-4716-4882-3

CONTENTS

1997

Rosen Trevithick

Since 2012 began, Rosen's books have sold over 28,000 copies. So far two titles have broken into Amazon's Top 100 Kindle Books chart and *Lipstick and Knickers* led the fictional comedy chart for almost three weeks.

Rosen was born in Cornwall, during the Chinese year of the sheep. She studied at Oxford before moving back to the West Country.

She now lives on the south coast of Devon with two imaginary cats, fantasising about getting a real one.

To find out more, visit http://rosentrevithick.co.uk

HOW COULD I have been so wrong? Anya walked into my record store at three-fifteen that afternoon, and five minutes later, she asked me out to dinner. The natural assumption was that she was attracted to me.

It was the summer of 1997, Oasis *"D'You Know What I Mean?"* was at number 1. Everybody was talking about *Fifth Element*, the first Austin Powers film and *Men in Black*. Princess Diana was still alive. In Falmouth, the bar and grill called Five

Degrees West, was still a pub called The Pirate, and it still hosted live music every night.

It was difficult to identify a lesbian in the late nineties. Loose fitting shirts, combat trousers and converse shoes were popular fashions for everybody. Anya was no exception. She looked particularly fetching in the current fashions but it was impossible to know whether her grungy outfit was a mark of the times, or lesbian tastes. She was naturally stunning, with Asian eyes and long, shiny black hair tied back in a lazy ponytail.

I was thirty-two. By day, I ran a record store and by night, I jammed with one of the many bands of the nineties called Crushed Velvet. We'd been together since school. Sometimes we played at The Pirate, supporting larger bands such as Feeder, Ash and Reef. I had a long-term crush on the lead singer from a local band called Thunderbirdz.

Cornwall was starting to succumb to the influences of the rest of England. Its first Body Shop opened in Truro in the early 90s and other chains started to follow. One or two gay bars were launched, decorated with informative screens, which displayed slide shows preaching about how committed the constabulary was to protecting "the Cornish gays". Each town had a token ethnic family.

It was so unusual to see a woman of Asian descent in Falmouth in 1997, that I knew I'd seen Anya before, although for the life on me, I couldn't remember where.

I wondered how many times she'd been into the record store before asking me out. Certainly, the purposeful way that she introduced herself suggested more than a brief moment's contemplation.

The twinkle in her eye seeded fantasies for the remainder of the afternoon. Eventually, I became too distracted to work and had to close up early.

Her invitation was delivered with the perfect combination of confidence and vulnerability. She asked, boldly enough, then stared at the ground, tickling a fingernail, as she waited for a response. I loved her deep, guttural voice, like her words were being driven over a gravel track.

I imagined how we'd look on a mattress together. Her dark locks mingling with my blonde "Rachel" do as she drew me in for a kiss... Her slender Eurasian figure pressing against my curvy body …

As I chose my dress for the date, I pitied all the days that a stunning customer hadn't asked me out. After trying on several outfits, a brown floral frock with green Doc Marten boots promised to do justice to the occasion.

For an insecure moment, I wondered if there was any chance that she might not turn up. Back then, only those who were both rich and very sturdy managed to carry mobile phones, which were costly and built like bricks. No, you had to go on faith alone. I reminded myself that *she* asked *me* out, the chances of being stood up were slim.

When I arrived at the restaurant, Anya was wearing the same shirt and trouser combo that she'd had on in the shop, but she'd applied smudged eyeliner for the occasion. This was bold in the late 90s, when "dare to be bare" (without being anything of the sort) was the facial cosmetics fashion.

We met at the Marina Bar and Restaurant, which was pretty upmarket for me. When I walked in she was already seated, I gave her my best dazzling smile. No point in being coy. We were two grown adults who were attracted to each other. Why spoil it with false modesty? I wondered how old she was. Her face was smooth and youthful, but her manner, and choice of restaurant, suggested she was in her early thirties, like me.

"Hello again! How was the rest of your day?" she asked.

"Destroyed by thoughts of you naked," I wanted to say, but I decided that that might be one step too far. "It went well. How about yours?"

"I got some chores done. Thankfully, I have Wednesdays off."

"What is it that you do?"

"I'm a life model. You know, for artists."

"How poetic! How modern! How brave!"

"Why thank you."

"So, where are you from? I couldn't help noticing that your features are not traditionally Cornish."

She chuckled and smiled. "I'm from London. The features that you may have noticed are from my mother. She was Chinese."

"*Was* Chinese."

"Yes, *was*. She passed away."

"I lost my mother too."

Anya was quiet for a moment. I wondered if we might bond on this common loss, but she rapidly changed the subject – which was probably a healthier direction for our relationship to take. "Now tell me about you! You own the record shop, right?"

"Yes."

"Do you sell many records these days?"

"No, it's mostly about CDs, but some enthusiasts won't touch them. There will always be a market for vinyl."

"Is it your passion, selling records? You seem like somebody who is more creatively inclined?"

"I'm in a band!"

I felt as though we'd known each other for years, even though we had only formally met today. I wondered whether the sex was going to work this well. Would she instinctively know my desires? I was a firm believer in what happens on the streets is reflected under the sheets.

"Tell me about your band. It sounds fascinating!"

"I play lead guitar. We all met in school – except the drummer, she joined later. We're an all-girl band. There is incredible chemistry between us – not like that though, I *am* single." I realised I'd announced my status rather too defensively, so I repeated with an air of forced breeze, "I'm single." That made it more subtle, right?

"What sort of music do you play?"

"Some covers – you know Elastica, Suede… And a few of our own."

"Have you got any gigs lined up?"

"There's one two weeks on Friday. You should come!"

"I'd love to!"

It was incredible. Anya wanted to know all about me; my work and my hobbies. She asked deep, meaningful questions about my life. She laughed at my jokes. She boasted a little – shy mentions of paintings sold and a poetry prize.

As we waited for the bill, I felt the familiar buzz of excitement that I always felt just prior to a night of frantic new-relationship sex. I beamed at Anya across the table. She smiled back, a little more shyly that I expected. Perhaps she wouldn't be as dominating as the vision my mind's eye had conjured.

I decided to wait until we were outside the restaurant for our first kiss. If there was ever a time and a place that a kiss between two girls could go by unnoticed in a restaurant, it was not 1997 Falmouth. Our first kiss should be a private moment, away from prying eyes.

She was a few jiffies behind me, collecting her coat. I felt my heart begin to race. No! I didn't need time to get nervous. I needed to act fast! I waited for her to take three steps, clearing her from the restaurant and prying diners, and then firmly, I put a hand on her waist and guided her toward me. I was surprised to find my embrace was met with more resistance that I expected. My lips searched for hers and I felt a little drunk on excitement.

"What are you doing?" she cried.

Suddenly, I was stone cold sober. Was she rejecting me? I couldn't believe she was rejecting me. She'd been working to impress me all night. What possible explanations were there besides romantic interest?

"I'm going to marry your father."

What?

This had to be a joke. My father doesn't date lesbians.

"I'm sorry; we wanted you to get to know me before we told you."

"*We?*"

"Yeah."

I stepped backwards into the shelter of the wall. Humiliated I let me weight transfer into the brickwork. It was fair to say that it was the most mortifying moment of my life. What could make it any worse?

"He doesn't know you're a lesbian, does he?"

* * *

I hadn't spoken to my father in three weeks. I preferred not to think about what he and the floozy might be up to. What sort of job was a nude model anyway? If she were as good at painting and poetry as her bragging suggested, she wouldn't need to demean herself to make money.

She was a ridiculous woman; far too showy to be taken seriously. She was making a fool out of him.

I could only imagine how ridiculous they looked together, him with his silver receding hair and her with a stupidly shiny oil slick pouring from her head.

There wouldn't be a wedding. It couldn't possibly be the sort of engagement that would result in a wedding. It was probably more like the kind of engagement that would involve the exchange of a couple cheekily-priced bits of jewellery and then fizzle out. The thought of that tart cheapening my father's distinguished reputation, made me sick.

He suited being a widower. It was appropriate for him to attend cancer charity fundraisers and accept lasagnas from concerned neighbours. It was not appropriate for him to attend pretentious restaurants and accept cheap and nasty sexual favours from a Thai bride.

I despised my inner racist and my total inability to tolerate Anya, but I didn't seem to be able to calm myself. She had humiliated me. She had gone about things in totally the wrong way. Perhaps if she'd done things differently, I'd find her easier to accept. This was all her fault.

The phone rang, as it often did. I didn't even bother to pause my *X Files* video. No way was I going to answer a call without knowing who was ringing. I was not stupid. I'd wait and then dial 1471. Relationships had become so much easier in the last three years, following the introduction of 1471.

By now, my dad must have heard about my sexuality. He probably wanted to talk about it or something utterly humiliating. Whilst many of my friends dreamt of their parents sitting them down and offering their full, wholehearted support, I dreamt of my coming out going by without remark or expression.

I was gay yesterday. I was gay today. Nothing had actually changed so there is no need for anybody to behave as though it had. Me being straight, now that *would* be remarkable.

However, my dad was one for drama. He'd called a family meeting when I got my first school detention and another when I got my first merit mark. No doubt he'll want to do a little pacing and some sharp breathing. Then it will become a reason for him to tell me how much I mean to him, on every family occasion, for now until eternity.

A quick call to 1471 did indeed reveal that it was my dad calling.

I let the phone ring again. Talking was the last thing I wanted to do.

The doorbell rang. I slumped downstairs in my Flying Dodo fleece and slippers. It was probably the new book I ordered on Amazon – some new writer called J.K. Rowling, who I thought I'd give a try. There was no chance that yet another book about witches and wizards would catch on, but it sounded like a little light reading for the beach.

The doorbell rang again. I checked that my pussy wasn't showing, and opened the door.

Anya.

I was about to close it again, when she put a foot in the door. I was a bit taken aback by such an aggressive move. I wished I'd put my jeans on. I tugged at my fleece to hide my bulging thighs.

"What do *you* want?"

"He's called off the engagement."

I did a smug shrug.

"Can I come in?"

"I'm not dressed."

"Well get dressed."

"No can do."

"Please can I come it?"

"No point really, is there. Now that you're not going to be my wicked stepmother after all." I started to close the door.

"You selfish cow."

I swung the door open. "Pardon?"

"You heard me."

"What have I done? I haven't even spoken to him."

"Exactly. He thinks that means you don't approve of me."

"I *don't* approve of you."

"Why not?"

"Do you need me to spell it out to you?"

"I was good enough for you."

"What?"

"You wanted me for yourself, but apparently I'm not good enough for your father."

"To fuck. I wanted you *to fuck.* I wasn't going to marry you, you dumb bitch." Even as I said it, I wondered what I was saying, but somehow I couldn't stop myself. The words just kept spilling out. *Dumb bitch.*

She had no more fight in her; she took her foot out of my hallway and retracted back into the road. "I didn't tell him you know."

"What?"

"I didn't tell him that you're gay."

I shrugged.

She started to walk away.

For some reason, I called after her, "Why not?"

It was her turn to shrug.

I watched her disappear into the distance. The remorse hit me immediately, but obviously not enough to convince me to go after her. I was certain that a woman almost half my father's age, would not make him happy in the long run. I would tolerate this temporary unpleasantness, in the name of his long-term happiness.

* * *

A week later, I was still fuming over the meeting with Anya – partly because I hated how she'd behaved, but mainly because of the things *I* had said. What had she turned me into?

Still, Crushed Velvet were playing tonight, so I could enjoy a few hours of escapism. Just me, the girls and a pub full of appreciative locals. It was exactly what I needed to take my mind off Anya.

I prayed that our band would not be supporting Thunderbirdz - not again. Not another hour spent gazing at the lead singer, wishing she would fall off the stage and into my pants.

My obsession with her had begun three months ago, when I'd first heard her sing. Her husky, rusky voice sent shivers down my spine and she had a presence that cried, "Move over Marilyn, history has a new Goddess". Since then, we'd tried every sex act known to man, in my head, and I could no longer look her in the eye.

Fortunately, I was rarely required to look her in the eye. We'd exchanged six words, ever. "Pass my whiskey!" and "The tall one?"

I wouldn't have minded having a little crush if I were sixteen, but here was I, a grown woman, lusting over a local singer as if I was a spotty teenage runt to her Justine Frischmann. I didn't do crushes. This was insane.

I got to The Pirate early. I was so used to it being full that it seemed like a desert without people. On the walls were blackboards sporting Simpsons cartoons and a depiction of Jim Carey in *The Mask*. I rarely got to enjoy the artwork, it was always so packed.

Trudy appeared from the toilets. "It's Thunderbirdz," she said.

"I told you to warn me if it was Thunderbirdz!" I whined. Already I could feel prickles on the back of my neck, as my heart rate increased. By my age, I'd learnt to dread the lust drug – it only leads to trouble.

Debbie Jones. Her name was plain enough, but there was nothing plain about the girl. She had scraggly "Meg Ryan" highlighted hair, cut to just below the ears, and even though it was short, it created a shimmering cloud as she tossed her head around on stage. She was skinny – much thinner than the girls I was usually attracted to, but had the stage presence of an energetic rhino.

I remembered her last gig with a smile. She'd been wearing a white lace top held together with safety pins. Friendship bracelets hugged her wrists. Baggy jeans, complete with dangling key chain, hung from her hips. Their low slung waist exposed the top of knickers with "Calvin Klein" printed on the elastic. What might she be wearing today?

"Karen!"

I spun around. Oh my God! There she was – Debbie Jones. The same low-slung jeans, but today with a distressed black tank top. I lost the power of speech. I just gawped at her. She knew my name!

"It is Karen, isn't it?"

"Yeah," I drawled, almost forgetting that words needed to be ended.

"I'm a big fan!"

"You are?" I could feel my heartbeat with the back of my ears.

"Yeah! I don't know why you're supporting us – you should be headlining!"

"No, you *deserve* to headline."

"No, you do."

"No, you do."

Trudy cut in, "Let's just say you both do."

"Can we catch up after the show?" asked Debbie.

I grinned like a demented frog. I couldn't find any words.

"Maybe we could get a drink?" she adds.

Another, gormless grin. Boom. My life as I knew it was over.

* * *

We took off our shoes at the start of the sand. It was almost pitch black but the noise of other people mapped out the dimensions of the beach. Apparently, half past twelve on an August evening was a popular time for visiting Gyllingvase beach.

We waded past numerous canoodling couples, who must have either felt that the darkness cloaked them, or didn't care.

We didn't care either. We just wanted to be together. Six months of playing at the same gigs, watching each other on the stage, wanting each other, had all built up to this moment, and nothing, not even two hundred strangers, was going to ruin it.

We fell down onto the sand and begun kissing. I ran my fingers through her hair, noting how soft it felt, not full of product like it appeared – natural funk. She put her hands around my waist and drew me closer. The soft introduction was short lived and we rapidly became more frantic, tearing at each other's clothes.

Having to maintain a baseline of discretion just made it all the more exciting. I hadn't had sex out of doors since I was a student. At least, having fantasised about this moment at least eight hundred times, I had plenty of tricks up my sleeve.

The seconds turned into minutes, the minutes turned into hours… Absolute bliss is timeless.

Before we knew it, the morning sun was shining down on us. I opened my eyes, not really sure whether I'd been asleep or not.

"Morning gorgeous!" she sung, taking the words right out of my mouth.

I grinned back. "Morning!" I still felt slightly tongue tied around her, even after the things we'd done last night. I forced myself to ask, "Can I see you again?"

"I hope so!" she grinned.

"How about Tuesday, we could go into Truro to see a film."

"Oh…"

"Well we don't have to."

"No, I want to. Let's do it."

"Really, if you don't want to…"

"No, I just hesitated because it's a school night, that's all."

I smiled, it's a fun expression, *school night*. "What is it that you do?"

"English, French, Geography and Sociology."

"Huh? For a *degree?*"

"No, those are the A-levels I'm doing."

A-levels? Shit! A-levels? No way. "How old are you?"

"Seventeen."

Fuck! "Oh."

"Is that a problem?"

Yes! "No."

"It is. It's a problem isn't it?"

"No, I was just surprised, that's all. I'm thirty-two."

"Wow! Really? No! You can't be. You're really in your thirties?"

"Is that a problem?

"No, I'm just surprised."

If I said I wasn't fazed by Debbie's age, I'd be lying. The revelation knocked me sideways. However, although age itself was just a number, there was no denying that the gap might build many obstacles of epic proportions.

I asked her, "Do you think this will work?"

"I don't know. I hope so."

"Me too."

I meant what I said. She may have been fifteen years younger than me, but it didn't change how I felt – how I'd felt about her for months. Perhaps we'd discover that our lives were just too different, that we wanted different things or that we couldn't get along with each other's friends. Potential problems popped into my mind in vast quantities, but they didn't change the overriding factor that I wanted to give it a go.

"What's the matter?" asked Debbie, as I pulled myself up from the sand.

"I have to go somewhere."

"It's the age isn't it?"

"No," I assured her, bending down and kissing her soft lips. "I *really* want to see you again. There's just something that I need to do."

* * *

"What's the matter Karen?" asked my Dad, looking alarmed. "You look like you've been dragged through a hedge backwards."

"Nah, nothing like that, just slept on the beach."

"You what?"

"Is Anya here?"

"No. We … we called off the engagement."

"I don't want you to!"

"Well it's happened now."

"Well make it unhappen!"

"Karen, would you like to come in?" He stepped to one side and I walked into the house he'd shared with my mother for thirty years. It was hard for me to imagine another woman living here. Was I really convinced that I wanted him to marry Anya? Had one night with a hot seventeen year old really changed my perspective on my entire family setup?

I looked at the couch my mother chose, the fireplace she used to polish, the photographs she had framed. Could I really stand to see Anya draped all over that sofa, looking at our family photos – joining them?

I took check of the situation. How long had I known Debbie? Was it really realistic to think that I'd changed my entire viewpoint based on as bit of mind-blowing sex?

But then again, maybe my viewpoint hadn't changed, maybe I'd just opened my eyes to a truth that I should have faced all along – my father deserved to move on. How odd that a girl so much younger than me could inspire me to grow up.

"I haven't seen you for a month."

"Sorry."

"Anya told me that you two had some kind of falling out."

"She came into the shop Dad. She pretended she was someone else."

"Really, who did she pretend to be?"

"Well… she didn't tell me you were engaged."

"I told her I thought it was the wrong way to go about things, but she's quite headstrong, just like you. Didn't you like her?"

"I did at first."

"And what changed your mind?"

"Did you really break up with her?"

"No, she left me."

"*She* left *you*?"

"Yes, she said she couldn't get in the way of a man and his daughter."

"Well go and get her back."

"It's not that simple."

"Why not?"

"Well, she's going back to London."

"London? That's what? Five hours away!"

"Then she's going to China for six months, to spend time with cousins."

"Well stop her!"

"What makes you think she'll change her mind?"

"It was never her standing in the way! It was me!"

"Well then, we'd better get over to Truro before her train leaves."

* * *

Like a scene from a cheesy movie, we rushed out of the front door, down the path and onto the road, where Dad's Volkswagen Jetta was parked. I knew Dad was loving the drama.

"What time is her train?" I asked.

"Three twenty-two."

"That's very specific."

"I've fantasised about this moment," he confessed.

Just then, in the rear-view mirror, I saw something that completely drained the situation of its natural suspense and thrill – Anya.

She was fast approaching, carrying nothing but her small Chanel handbag. Presumably, she'd changed her mind about travelling. I felt weird. There were conflicted knots in my stomach.

Dad started to pull away.

"Wait!" I cried.

"What is it? Don't say you've changed your mind."

"*I* haven't changed my mind."

Dad looked around at Anya. She was wearing a white t-shirt and charcoal pedal- pushers. Her beautiful black hair shone it the sun.

I could pinpoint the exact moment that Anya noticed that I was in the car. Her expression changed from one of hope and expectation, to despair and then she put on a stubborn poker face, giving nothing away about the final stages of her emotional transformation.

"She couldn't go!" cried Dad. I could swear his eyes were welling up a little, but tried not to believe it. I'd never seen my father get gooey about a woman.

I watched as he hurriedly got out of the car.

"I forgot my passport," she said, standoffishly.

It was my father's turn to drain of optimism.

I opened the passenger door and climbed out. "It's all right," I told Anya.

She looked at me with me and raised an eyebrow.

"It's all right. You have my blessing. Marry the old fool."

Anya turned to my dad and muttered, "Is she serious?"

Dad nodded.

Anya paused for a second and then threw her arms around me. She smelt of strawberries and for an uncomfortable moment I remembered our dinner "date". Slowly, the resentment started to creep back.

Then, I thought of Debbie and the unlikely happiness that we'd found together in such a small time. I may have been riding on the crazy high of new romance, but coming to terms with my father remarrying wasn't easy and I needed whatever help I could get.

When Anya let go of me, she turned to Dad and flung her arms around his neck. It was weird to watch and I felt a sudden pang as I was reminded of Mum.

She turned back to me. "So, you'll come to the wedding?"

"Of course," I smiled. It was hard for me to say, but I recognised that it was something I had to do.

It was Dad's turn to speak. "Thank you," he said, hugging me.

"I want you to be happy," I told him.

"I want me to be happy!" he laughed. "But you also …"

"Actually Dad, I am seeing somebody. It's early days and it depends how things go, but I might bring Debbie."

"Debbie?" he says, mulling it over for a few moments. "Is she a …" I braced myself for a speech, but when my father opened his mouth again, it was to ask, "Is she a vegetarian?"

***

Five Guns Blazing

Emma Rose Millar

Emma Rose Millar is a single mother who lives in the Midlands with her young son. She studied for a degree in Humanities with the Open University and now works part-time as an interpreter. She is currently writing her first novel for Freya Publications.

THE BOSTON TIMES, November 18th, 1720

Wanted pirates Anne Bonny, Mary Read and John 'Calico Jack' Rackham have been captured by pirate hunter Jonathan Barnet and sentenced to death by the Jamaican Governor. In accordance with British Common Law both women were granted a temporary stay of execution having pleaded their bellies, and being quick with child. Rackham was at the hour of ten this morning hung by the neck until he was dead. Captain Barnet faced little resistance from the murderous outlaws save Bonny and Read who fought viciously with another unknown pirate while the remainder of the crew slept like drunken dogs. It seems the vagabond Rackham preferred his women to do his dirty work in the end.   The King has offered a reward for information leading to the arrest of this mystery pirate.

***

My mother was well acquainted with the good magistrates of Holborn, such was her propensity for relieving wealthy gentlemen of their belongings; handkerchiefs, pocket watches, etcetera. After her third sentence and extremely narrow escape from the gallows it was deemed she had not the means to provide for herself and we were sent to the workhouse to be fed and clothed and instructed in the ways of Christian honesty.   It was upon our incarceration in that house of orphans that my mother had the foresight to disguise me as a boy, Nathaniel Beedham so as to protect me from the advances of the squire and the beadle and anyone else who might take a fancy to me and I was set to work in the mill which was backbreaking work indeed for a little girl of only ten.   We were clothed, albeit in the most raggedy garb and fed a diet of gruel, clear soup of some kind and bread with a slice of meat or cheese on Sundays, but still this was not enough for my mother who had a taste by then for the finer things in life. She had succumbed to the temptations of tobacco and gin and she stole a shilling from the church collection plate, the crime of which won for us the favour of being transported to the plantations of Barbados; I would never set foot on British shores again.

We sailed from Portsmouth on the King's ship *Redemption,* who was tossed around like a matchbox on the crashing Atlantic waves. Unrelenting winds lashed against the good ship, lifting its bow from the ocean while the captain fought to bring it under control. Rations on board were no better than those from the workhouse kitchen; hard biscuits, salt pig and lemons to combat the scurvy which blighted our seamen. The sickness in my belly staved off my hunger, which was just as well as my mother ate half my share. She explained it to me well though, "If you fatten Laetitia then your monthly curse might be upon you," I was shocked suddenly at hearing her call me by my female name, "We will need such swathes of bandages under your breeches to disguise it. I will have to stay buxom if I am to hope that a planter shall marry me."

The voyage lasted seventy gruelling days during which time my mother's luggage was looted by a crewmember that she kicked in the shin upon discovering the thief. Later she was held fast by two of the captain's crew while a third tore open her dress and punched and kicked her so hard that the skin beneath her eye split open and she fell with blood streaming from her face. As she lay there with her cheek pressed against the deck she looked up at me and said, "Boy! Don't you ever let anyone treat you like that, learn to fight like a man do you hear me?"

I nodded, "Yes Mother."

Then as I looked up I saw the most beautiful thing, I saw land, the beaches of Barbados gleaming so white that I first thought it was snow, which had drifted in on the warming breeze and now lay glistening with frost as if diamonds had been strewn over its surface. Behind it sat a canopy of trees, their foliage so dense that the air beneath it was damp and cool. Then there was the sun, a glorious red sun, which sank low down on the horizon where the ocean met the clouds, and the sky melted around it in tones of magenta and violet. I turned so that my face would be bathed in its glow and my heart was gladdened. I remembered as a little girl the beadle regaling tales of heaven from the Old Testament, this was it; this was my heaven…but not for long.

We were lined up on the beach and sold to the planters; my mother and I as a pair, sold with the African slaves, but we were so much luckier than they, we were free from shackles, we were sold only for the terms of our redemptions, (seven years in our case) and carried with us magistrate's papers, outlining the terms under which we were to be kept; we were to be provided each with two suits of clothing, given meat or fish once a week, taught to read from a bible and the working day should not exceed twelve hours during which there would be a break for nourishment. The beadle was to reside on the island to oversee conditions. But who was to intervene on behalf of the slaves? Only God it seemed and, as far as I could see, He was not doing a very good job. In all my life I never saw such horror as I saw that day in the eyes of those people lined up and paraded like cattle before the planters on the beach.

Only the poorest and most short-sighted of planters bought the British labour; we were cheaper than the slaves owing to the terms of our internment. My mother and I were sold to Mr and Mrs Lynch, sugar planters who prided themselves on the fair treatment of their workers who were put out to toil in gangs. My mother was dressed well so that the planters could demonstrate their benevolence to their friends and set to work as a maid in the house, a two-storey residence with sprawling out buildings in which the workers slept, as large as Holborn jail and with an open porch running along the width of the ground floor and a series of rectangular windows, often left open to allow in the fresh breeze while the screens behind them kept insects out. I was put out on the plantations and assigned the tasks of clearing land, holing, planting, weeding, boiling and cane cutting. Muscles grew on my shoulders and across my back so that when I raised my arms to swing my scythe I resembled a cobra from behind. I worked under the scorching glare of the sun, which shone yellow in the cloudless sky. I had never seen a sky so blue, not in London anyway when even in summer a misty haze spread across the heavens while the pale sun fought its way through like a distant star. Conditions for me were no worse than in the workhouse mill and at least I was away from the freezing cold of Holborn with its collapsing buildings and the stench in the labyrinth of alleyways, which concealed criminals at their every turn.

Towards the end of our internment came the event of my seventeenth birthday; on the eve of which my mother was permitted to take me to the Peacock Tavern, where planters ate fish outdoors and Barbadian women danced under the lamplights. It was a world away from the seedy taverns of Holborn; those damp cellars with their syphilitic drunks and toothless crones. We sat outside drinking sugared rum as the warm evening breeze swirled gently around us under a sky of indigo speckled with stars and a silver moon so thin that it seemed as if a machete blade had ripped through the heavens.

It was then that I first saw the pirate Rackham with my mother sitting drunk on his knee, "He could be your footman," she was saying, "he is strong as an ox and will work as hard as any slave." The gentleman looked disinterested but she persevered, "she is a girl," she whispered and I was sold to the good gentleman for five guineas.

"I will not hurt you Beedham," smiled Rackham, "not unless you especially want me to." He was a handsome man with skin the colour of honey and hair and eyes both of such a dark shade of brown that they were almost black.

He took me aboard his ship, *Revenge,* a double-masted narrow sloop large enough for seventy men with a battery of five cannons along the broadside. By day I was entrusted with the tasks of scrubbing the decks, raising and lowering sails as the Caribbean winds dictated and keeping the hull clean of seaweed, shellfish and other marine-life so as not to slow our progress. The shallow draft of the vessel allowed us to hide in the shoal waters concealed in coves, which the larger warships were too big to enter, and we could outrun them too, reaching speeds sometimes of up to eleven knots. By night I would attend to Rackham's other needs. The gentleman did not use me too ill, he took me always from behind, but as a woman, not as a boy if you understand my meaning, and always with my breaches on; he'd had a Barbadian seamstress sew me a false gusset which could quickly be unbuttoned as he desired. My breasts always remained bound under my shirt, although I must own there was little to bind. I never, ever undressed, in case others of the crew should enter the room and discover my sex. Women were not permitted on the ship, although I later found that Rackham was maverick with this rule, as he was with many others. Being found with a young man would not have been so bad, lots of pirates kept them, indeed there was talk abound that the King himself kept a man-servant.

My hopes of swashbuckling and blazing guns, of cavalier dare-devilishness and the clashing of swords were soon quashed, "I am tired Beedham… and I am old," (he was thirty-seven.) We have been offered a pardon from Governor Rogers and I am going to accept it. I am hoping he will offer me a commission to plunder and take the Spanish ships, but moreover I am hoping it is not a trick and he will have me captured and I will swing from the gallows with my feet twitching." I felt myself grow cold, "Anyway, we will wait; there is one more person we need to take with us, another pirate who is to receive the pardon. I will know when the time is right and then I shall fetch them from the tavern by the coast."

I kept Rackham closely in my sights as much as I could, so intrigued was I by the news of this nameless pirate, then one night he scrubbed himself at his sink and had me shave his chin close with his blade and he stole out into the night while he thought I was sleeping. I stalked him through the shadows, through the chorus of crickets and the song of Magnolia Warblers with the soft sand beneath my feet and the balmy air warming my skin. I followed him right down to the tavern and that was when I saw her, she was the most beautiful woman I saw in all my life, with hair the colour of saffron tumbling in wild waves around her elbows and her eyes as blue as the Caribbean sea. My own hair was as red as a cherry, and coarse, hanging much shorter in its tight ringlets and my eyes were as pale as a glacier. My skin was scorched and freckly; hers like Venetian marble, and the way she spoke and tossed her head around! All those about her fell quiet. It was more than that I admired her; I wanted to be that woman, I wanted her to devour me just so I could be a small part of her.

"Ha Rackham! Your notoriety comes from lies; tell them the truth, you made your career plundering paddle boats close to shore!"

He just laughed at her, "My ships off Bermuda say different! She is beautiful is she not gentlemen? Any man who has a wife so beautiful should slice her face; it is the only way to keep her chaste!"

"The last person who made a threat like that ended up with a knife in their belly," she smiled, "Would you like me to stab you Jack?"

"If you don't come here and kiss me right now I might just stab you!" he retorted to much laughter among the men, and she did, she went right over and kissed him and I skulked off into the night like a wounded dog. It was not only that Jack had never kissed me, though I supposed my breath was rank enough, it was that I wanted to be one to kiss her, to taste her lips. I spent the night on the beach under an up-turned fishing boat with a web of confusion weaving its way through my mind.

***

"What are you doing Beedham?" asked Rackham gruffly. He had crept up behind me the following afternoon as I scrubbed the decks with the burning sun on my back. His shadow loomed long over the plank, "And why on earth are you dressed like that?"

I had cut a hole in the top of my hat and soaked my hair in lemon juice so that the sun might lighten it like hers, and rubbed coconut oil into my skin to soften it.

"And why did you not come back last night?"

"I saw you," I replied quietly, unable even to look at him, "with a beautiful lady and I presumed you would need your privacy."

"Ah Beedham you are jealous! That's so sweet. As for the lady, she is no lady, she is my wife Beedham, the pirate Anne Bonny, and I should like you attend to her in our quarters. Do whatever she asks."

"Yes Sir." I gave a little curtsey.

"And Beedham… Don't ever spy on me again."

***

While bound for the Bahamas I knocked on Rackham's door and let myself in, "At your service my lady," I said falling into a deep bow. She lay on Rackham's bed in only her undergarments with her supple limbs spread out gracefully. I was suddenly embarrassed of my boyish attire and of that bed which had not been changed since my arrival.

"At my service really?" she teased, "Let me see, you are a very attractive boy, perhaps there is one thing you could do for me; perhaps you could kiss me. She reached up and stroked my cheek.

I caught her hand, "I am not a boy," I whispered, "I am a girl; my name is Laetitia Beedham."

"Yes I know," she smiled, "And Jack knows that I know; he is a puerile soul; really quite infantile! I'll wager the two of you have been playing with guns like two schoolboys!"

It was true; from almost the moment of my arrival he had proudly shown off his weaponry, "This is a volley-gun Beedham, a pistol. You do not have to be such a good shot to fire one of these; they will shoot a dotted line across a man's chest, but make sure at least one barrel hits them; they take an age to reload!" He showed me how to pistol-whip with a flintlock and instructed me on the use of a cutlass in the confined spaces below deck.

"Told you!" cried Anne, "He has all the sophistication of a twelve year old! The thought of two women together excites him. Does it excite you too Beedham?"

"I don't know," I said with a blush extending right down to my collarbones.

"Well perhaps this might make up your mind for you," she said, and she stood up, grabbed my shirt in her fist and kissed me; her lips were soft and I stood there shaking not knowing whether to touch her.

45

"You are trembling," she giggled.

"I am shy," I told her "Nobody has ever kissed me before."

"What? Jack does not kiss you?" Then she bit her bottom lip and her eyes were on fire, "Is he very cruel?"

"No!" I cried sharply and a look of bitter disappointment washed over the good lady's face. Jack had slapped me once, for toying with his musket whilst he was on deck, and it had hurt too; his hands were like spades, but afterwards he was so guilt ridden that he retreated to the kitchens directly, bringing back with him a wedge of goose pie and a plate of sliced fruits in recompense.

"Oh well," she said, almost sadly and then she kissed me again, shook my hair loose and slowly undressed me. Her tiny hand glided gently around my waist while the other was within her own undergarments and I grabbed hold of her wrist with a look of protestation; save my mother no human being had ever seen me naked and I was suddenly ashamed of my skinny frame, "My word that's a strong grip you've got Beedham!"

She took my hand gently and ran it over the smooth white skin of her bosom and belly, let it steal slowly up her soft leg and then squeezed it between her thighs until sliding through my arms she sank to the floor with her breast rising and falling and her head thrown backwards, her hands clasped around her lovely neck.

Afterwards, we lay sleeping with our faces almost touching and our arms entwined way late into the evening until Rackham came back drunk and stinking of rum with his face dark with anger. The door flew open with a bang and he stood there crookedly, steadying himself. "Get out Beedham!" he thundered while I scrabbled to my feet, snatching my clothes from the floor, then he threw me out naked into the corridor and I slid across the planks with my breeches clutched to my chest.

"Whatever is the matter Jack?" I heard her say in her soft Celtic burr.

"Governor Rogers, that's what," he yelled.

"He granted you the pardon surely?" she said lowering her voice, "otherwise you would not be here now."

"Oh yes! He granted me the pardon, but no commission. He doesn't trust me to bring down the Spaniards apparently. What in God's name does he expect the crew to live on? Get away from the door Beedham!" but I took no notice and continued behind it, with my ear pressed against the splintered wood.

"I have an idea," said the lady, her voice no more than a whisper. "There is a ship, a sloop anchored off the north coast of Jamaica with a crew of only nine, but it is heavy with sugar and spices and gold. We could take it easily."

Rackham thought for a second, "I don't know Madam, how small is it? Could it outrun us? That is my reservation here."

"I would suggest we first befriend the crew, ask them to join us, then attack them in the dead of night when they least expect it, but bury some of our treasure along the coast beforehand, lest the hand of fate should guide us disastrously and we need to jump ship."

"Do not speak of things going awry Anne; I cannot conceive of it."

But the *Revenge* was turned around anyway, bound for the Jamaican coast. We arrived at Dry Harbour Bay just as the rays of the golden sun began to fan outwards from beneath the horizon. Even at this early hour the port was bursting with ships laden with sugar, pimento and arrowroot, which dawdled in the shallow western back reef. On the skirts of the mountains nestled the shops of Jewish settlers stocked with haberdashery, leatherwear and jewellery. Beyond them were farms breeding pigs and goats, and the vile plantations manned by an ever-increasing deluge of African slaves, brought in according to the orders of some of the most sickening individuals in history. Then there it was, the sloop ship *Fancy,* bobbing gently on the tide; the whole of the crew must have been below deck; it creaked eerily like a ghost ship.

We stayed anchored just off the coast until nightfall when the moon rose high over the *Revenge* with its craters clearly visible in its glowing silver light. Long after the market traders packed away their wares and the gannets finished screeching, Rackham and Bonny stole off into the darkness carrying a chest between them, Jack with a shovel slung over his shoulder. They looked furtively around them with the nervousness of thieves but still they did not see me sneaking silently behind them in the shadows. They came to a stop beside an enormous anchor, which had been thrust into the sand, a trophy most probably from a taken Spanish ship, left to perish in the salty tides under the merciless sun. It was as tall easily as a man and must have taken at least twelve privateers to haul it ashore. To the left of it Rackham began frantically digging, with beads of sweat glistening on his brow and the chest was lowered into the hole. Then I saw the lady Anne Bonny scrabbling with her fingers, covering the secreted chest like a dog burying his bone. I winced as she kissed him and then ran inland leaving him alone on the shifting sands.

Anne remained absent from the *Revenge* for three days while Rackham got drunk, terrorised fishermen and could not be prevailed upon to eat. Eventually she returned with a handful of new crew members, escapees mostly from the plantations, redemptioners and maroons, and a lady, dressed in breeches though her bosom was so ample that there was not a soul among us who could be fooled into thinking she was a man. As soon as he saw her, Rackham's eyes rolled upwards and he exhaled pointedly.

"Who is she Sir?" I asked upon noticing his irritation.

"My wife's friend," he sighed heavily, "The pirate Mary Read."

***

At dinner the whole crew sat around a huge rectangular wooden table eating roasted hog and stewed goat, washed down with flagons of beer. Rackham and I sat at one end, Anne and Mary at the other. I hated Mary on sight; she was perhaps ten years my senior and the spitefulness of her character was written all over her face. Her nose was so snub that it pulled her upper lip into a bow, revealing her blackened teeth. Her hair was brown and knotted and her eyes a mottled shade of green. She sat without shame with her head resting on my lady's shoulder, hanging on her every word. I felt a wave of jealousy wash over me; Anne did not once look my way, it was as if she did not even know me. At one point Rackham approached them and his wife waved him away like an unwanted servant. He just stood rooted to the spot, not knowing what he should do next. I at last went over to him and took him gently by the elbow, "Come on Rackham, let us retire to bed."

"Oh look!" cried Mary, "It's your little pet Bonny; how kind of Rackham to buy her for you. And she disguises herself as a boy too, though I'll wager she does not take much disguising! Tell me Rackham; are you very jealous of her? He was jealous of me Beedham, wanted me killed until he caught me in a state of undress in his wife's room and discovered my sex. He quite liked it after that!"

I could not help myself; I dragged Mary Read to her feet and punched her as hard as I could in her stomach, leaving her gasping for breath.

"Beedham!" Jack was furious, "I should have you whipped for that! Remember your place Beedham, you will show some respect to my wife's companion!"

He dragged me to his quarters and slammed me against the door, then he smiled at me and kissed me on the mouth, and he undressed me and made love to me with my ankles crossed behind his buttocks and my thighs shaking. But the moment we had finished we both looked into each other's eyes with bitter disappointment. Both of us knew that the other had been thinking of somebody else, of the blue-eyed Bonny Anne.

Later that night, as the crew slept I sat up on deck gazing into the stars and thinking of how different things might have been had my mother not sold me for a few gold coins. I would not have changed it for the world. Then suddenly, from the depths of the Jamaican night came a glow of flickering orange, floating towards our ship on the tide.

"Fire-boat!" My words were little more than a whisper, "Fire-boat!"

I rushed down below deck and tried to rouse the men, most of them lying drunk in a haze of spiced rum. I hammered on Rackham's door and flung it open to find the three of them in bed together, Jack, Mary and Anne, but I had not the time for jealousy. "There is a fire-boat Sir, coming right towards us."

"Somebody must have informed the authorities of our plan Rackham!" cried Mary glaring right at me, "Somebody close to us."

"Do not blame me! I would never…"

"Oh Rackham, she has done it for jealousy can you not see? She is jealous of you, she is jealous of Anne; she is madly in love with you both!"

"Silence!" raged Rackham, "I cannot think Madam with your constant prattling."

It was too late though; the fire-boat, with its cargo of sizzling iron bombs packed with explosives had struck broadside, tearing a hole the size of a small fishing vessel in the sloop, sending water flooding in and plumes of purple smoke pouring out. Flames licked upwards towards the decks with such ferocity that no man could get near the cannons, rendering them utterly useless. We were completely surrounded by Governor Lawes' men who threw boarding hooks on deck and climbed in swarms onto the *Revenge*. I managed with my axe to cut one of their lines sending a handful of them crashing back down onto the waves, and I fired blindly into the darkness, a blunderbuss in each hand. I don't know where Rackham sloped off to, but suddenly Bonny and Read were alongside me, firing at Lawes' men, our five guns blazing, but we didn't stand a chance; we were overwhelmingly outnumbered. I later heard that Bonny had shot our own men below deck for indolence and cowardice. She climbed desperately up the mast, I don't know why; to escape to the heavens I suppose, but her skirts tangled around her legs and Lawes' men hacked down the mast with their boarding axes. Even as she was captured her eyes were wild with glee and her hair danced around her face like a halo of fire.

I jumped ship and swam pell-mell for Dry Harbour Bay.

"I have come to see Anne Bonny," I explained to the jailer, "so that I might read to her from my bible."

He thought for a moment and then allowed me inside.

"Oh my God! Rackham!" He had been beaten to a pulp and lay shackled.

"Indeed Beedham, it is a shame to see him here, but then if he had fought like a man he might not have to be hung like a dog," said Bonny disdainfully. There was hardly a scratch on her. "And you Beedham! Jumping ship like a rat! But then I suppose you would not have been able to come here now and save me. Do you know what you are to do Beedham? We have to make it look convincing if we are to get away with it. When you get out of here you are to come and join me in South Carolina; go to Main Street, Charles Town, my family are well known there; they are wealthy and will look after you until we can be together. Are you ready Beedham?"

Before I had even nodded my head she had punched me in the guts, knocking the wind right from me. I saw that familiar look of rapture I had seen in her eyes twice before. Her fists came at me from every angle and I felt my lip split and my ribs crack under their blows. It was Rackham in the end who implored, "For pity's sake Madam leave her! Can't you see she has had enough?" She struck me anyway once more for luck and I fell to the floor in a convulsion while she removed my dress and slipped it on over her head. Then she stepped over me like I was a piece of muck and walked out of the jail with my bible under her arm.

As I lay on the floor, I saw my mother's face on the deck of the *Redemption* and I heard her voice saying "Don't you ever let anyone treat you like that, learn to fight like a man!" and I felt thoroughly ashamed.

"Listen to me Beedham," whispered Rackham once I was sufficiently restored, "there is treasure hidden in the port."

"I know Sir, beside the anchor, I ransacked it this morning; fear not, I left most of its contents untouched, just pilfered a few gold coins for my dress; I still have enough I think for my passage to America."

"Not that one! God, Anne will be digging it up as we speak! There is a tree, twenty yards to the rear of the anchor; you cannot miss it, the others are lush and green but this tree is dead to its roots, it is parched and twisted and its branches are bare. I have left something inside its trunk for you… You are not going to America though surely Beedham? She will use you ill, eat away at your very soul and then when she has finished with you she will discard you like a piece of rubbish. Promise a condemned man you will not go."

"If it pleases you Sir," I said, but I had every intention of sailing immediately to America.

I fell asleep that night with Rackham in my arms and was roused the following morning by the executioner and the Governor who had come to take him to the gallows.

"My goodness Madam!" cried the latter, "Whatever have they done to you?" and then turning to the executioner, "See that this woman gets a hot meal and sufficient clothing to cover her modesty, and be sure that the press don't get hold of this! Am I forever to be remembered as an imbecile who let the most notorious pirate of the Caribbean simply walk out of jail? Rackham, I should have your belly slit for this as you swing!"

***

I stood on the glistening sands of Dry Harbour Bay, its warmth between my toes, queuing with the other passengers, while the King's ship *Atonement* sliced its way through the ocean with the bubbling spray curling away from its bow. I turned my face from the burning sun and as I did I saw the dead tree stood decaying in the sand. I picked up my skirts and walked over to it, thrusting my hand into its hollow trunk and pulled out a purse, which was full of gold coins. Also in the purse was a curled up piece of paper:

"Dear Beedham,

You were always more to me than a convict's daughter who I bought for a few gold coins, you do know that don't you

Beedham? Keep me in your prayers that God may have mercy on my soul. Jack."

The *Atonement* slid into port, casting a shadow right across the bay. Then something took hold of me and I ran for my life towards the mountains. I was not a commodity to be bought and sold, I was no convict's daughter; I was a free woman with a pocket full of gold and with no plans but to let the sun warm my face and the calm waters bathe my feet.

***

REFERENCES

http://brethrencoast.com/Ship.html

www.rootsweb.ancestry.com/~brbwgw/ArticleSlavery18thCentury.html

http://forums.canadiancontent.net/history/48176-18th-century-london-its-daily.html

http://en.wikipedia.org/wiki/Calico_Jack

http://en.wikipedia.org/wiki/Redemptioner

http://www.thepiratesrealm.com/pirate%20weapons.html

http://www.portcities.org.uk/london/server/show/conMediaFile.985/Convicts-being-rowed-outto-a-prison-hulk.html

Break Away

Niamh Murphy

Niamh Murphy lives in the historic town of Colchester where she can indulge her passion for archaeology and history. She loves travelling and a recent trip to Cornwall was the inspiration for her story 'Break Away'. Her greatest ambition is to own a medieval castle, complete with turrets, towers and a drawbridge. She is terrified of Ewoks. To find out more visit www.niamhmurphy.co.uk

SHE DRAGGED IT along the cobbles.

Having wheels meant the damned case was supposed to be easier to manage but it insisted on veering off into passing strangers.

Sarah had been led to believe that St Ives was a quiet Cornish fishing village, an artistic retreat, a quaint idyll. Instead it was hot, loud and thronging with people.

Debbie had, of course, let her down. Apparently she couldn't get away from Tom and the kids. Sarah hadn't bothered to read the whole e-mail, she'd just got on the train and decided to make the most of the weekend alone. But so far she was struggling to have fun.

When she finally reached the B&B she was sweaty, irritated, tired and ready to collapse.

She'd imagined the landlady as a scatty, old cat lady, with long purple scarves who only rented out rooms for the company, as she'd inherited a fortune and now wiled away her days painting abstracts and quoting poetry.

But she couldn't have been more wrong.

The woman who opened the door was wearing a pair of figure hugging black jeans and a white shirt, her black hair had a slight curl to it and hung loose about her shoulders in a way that reminded Sarah of a painting she'd once seen. Her eyes were a beautiful bright green and her bare feet were the only hint that she was even slightly bohemian.

"Miss Deal?" Sarah asked, trying to stifle her surprise.

"Call me Jen" she smiled brightly putting out her hand "are you here about the room? Only I thought there were two of you."

Sarah's throat dried up, she wanted to say '*my secret lover can't get away from her husband this weekend so it's just little old me I'm afraid'* instead she mumbled something about problems at work.

"Well not to worry, would you like to come and see your room? Oh and mind the cactus. I have no idea why I left it there."

A day at an art gallery was just the peace and quiet she needed. It would give her a chance to think, contemplate and look at pretty things.

She was still angry at Debbie and hadn't responded to the late night text offering excessive apologies and a promise to 'make up for it'. She was being made a fool of. She was so angry at herself for putting up with it and so angry with Debbie for making her feel guilty.

She was lost in thought when she caught sight of Jennifer Deal staring at a colourful portrait of a Rhino balancing on a lemon. She hoped to squeeze past unnoticed; the last thing she needed was Jennifer's sunny disposition and those distractingly entrancing green eyes.

"Sarah!" *'Bugger'*

"Jennifer! I didn't see you there!" The lie slithered off her tongue like a well-oiled snake.

"Oh it's Jen, please call me Jen. Jennifer is so formal. I didn't expect to see you inside on a gorgeous day like today, why aren't you out frolicking on the beach?"

'Frolicking?'

"Well I'm not really one for the crowds, or the heat, or the beach come to think of it."

Jen laughed and leaned forward, conspiratorially.

"Well I think you might have come to the wrong place!"

Sarah forced a smile and tried to think of a polite way of telling her to sod off.

"Come on I'll take you down to the beach and get you an ice cream. You look like you could do with cheering up."

She didn't want to be cheered up. She wanted to look at art and tell herself she was taking her mind off things whilst wallowing in self-pity and hate. But as she looked at those eyes, that smile and the soft black hair tucked delicately behind her ear, she felt herself melting and mumbled 'ok'.

Jen chattered away as she led Sarah down to the long white beach stretching along the horizon, the bright blue sky reflected in the clear water and the sound of waves was lost beneath a cacophony of shouting, screaming, and laughter.

Suddenly she was handed an ice-cream with a chocolate flake. She hadn't even noticed Jen getting it.

"Oh you didn't have to!" She said as the ice cream started dripping onto her hand.

"My pleasure!" She took hold of Sarah's arm and led her down to the sea. "Now tell me Miss Sparks, and I do have to say that is a marvellous name, why have you travelled all the way down to lovely, sunny, practically-tropical, Cornwall only to wander round an art gallery looking like you've just been slapped?"

'Because I have just been slapped!' She thought, every time Debbie set her up then let her fall it was like a hard backslap across the face.

"I've always hated my name." She said, sidestepping the question.

"Really? Why? I think it's a brilliant name! Miles better than 'Deal', which might as well be 'Dull'."

"I nearly changed it once."

Jen looked at her with abject horror.

"NO! You can't! I love your name. I'd marry you just to get your name." Her tone suddenly changed. "Of course there would be other reasons to marry you as well, I mean, I'm sure there would be other reasons to marry you, I mean… I should shut up now." It was the first time she'd seen Jen flustered and it felt great to realise that this gorgeous girl must have a crush on her.

But because she didn't think she deserved to feel great and because it was far too complicated to be liked by this girl, she decided to crush this crush. Immediately.

"I'm just upset that my girlfriend isn't here, you know. I really miss her." She looked at Jen, testing her reaction.

"Of course you do," Jen said; calmly and without any trace of disappointment or the good humour she'd had a few seconds before.

'Not so flippin' cheery now are we!?' Sarah thought, with twisted satisfaction and then immediate guilt and regret as she realised she actually liked her cheeriness.

"Do you want to go surfing?" Jen asked suddenly.

"Surfing?" She couldn't conceal her disdain.

"Yeah, only I've got a class later and it would be great if you could come."

Sarah desperately wanted to make up for that fleeting desire to crush her. Besides if Jen was taking a class she couldn't be that good, so it's not as if she could make a fool of herself.

She was wrong.

"I thought you meant" she hissed as Jen walked over "that you were taking a class, not that you were *taking* a class!"

"Does it matter? Now get down on that board" she said with unexpected authority "and let me see you jump."

The next few hours passed awkwardly. It was fine watching demonstrations; Jen's athletic body moved with elegance and even when she came off she did so with the grace of a Russian gymnast. Sarah, however felt like a slightly unbalanced turtle in the midst of a group of synchronised dolphins. She felt like she was the only one struggling to get the knack of it and all she managed to achieve when she got in the water was a face full of sea. After the fortieth wipe-out she was exhausted and utterly powerless to get back on the board. Suddenly Jen was behind her. Sarah gasped as she felt gentle hands on her waist, they were comforting and warm but unexpected and she was surprised by her desire to be held tighter.

"Just hold it steady, jump, then slide on. Ready?" In a blind panic Sarah leapt on the board, which promptly flipped her backwards and straight into the sea.

She went under, just for a moment but long enough for water to get sucked up her nose, her arms flailed but she managed to stand up quickly, still in panic-mode. Jennifer was next to her and although she'd been under as well, she laughed, a warm, heartfelt laugh.

"I'm no good at this." Sarah said, with more acceptance than defeat, and by the look on Jen's face it was clear she agreed.

"Well technically the class ended about ten minutes ago so no-one would think any worse of us if we called it a day."

The offer was too tempting to refuse and they walked back up to the house in their surf gear. Sarah was able to have a shower, get into some warm clothes and come downstairs in time to be served a gorgeous looking casserole.

"I know it's not traditional seaside fare but I thought that, after today, you could do with something a bit more wholesome."

"Oh I'm *not* complaining!" She said as she took the seat next to Jen and they chatted about their afternoon.

She liked hearing Jen laugh, she liked watching her as she talked and when she giggled she sat back in her chair and occasionally moved her hand up to cover her mouth, a move that Sarah found both sweet and elegant.

It seemed natural for the evening to continue with a bottle of wine and relocation to the sofa. Sarah's itinerary of local pubs and live music was quickly dropped in favour of staying in and watching Jen laugh, talk and then laugh some more.

The normally reserved Sarah put on a more tactile persona, placing her hand on Jen's arm at the punch-line of a joke or an intimate detail in a story. She wanted to be nearer to Jen, closer to this beautiful girl. But as they finished off the bottle, Sarah felt her moment was slipping away.

"Are you ok?" Jen must have noticed the look of concern.

She smiled and nodded, not taking her eyes from Jen's, she wanted to say something but there were no convenient words. Instead she reached up and pushed back a loose lock of hair, her heart was throbbing in her chest as she stroked the soft skin of Jen's cheek.

Jen didn't back off and she didn't flinch; she looked at Sarah with unbroken gaze and then moved forward. They stared at one another, just a fraction apart, before finally they gave in and their lips brushed softly against one another.

Then the doorbell went.

Sarah recognised the voice of the woman talking to Jen at the door but she was still shocked when she emerged into the room. Her hair was perfect and her bright red lips matched her bright red nails, which matched her bright red luggage and her bright red scarf, which was draped dramatically around her shoulders.

"Debbie! You came?" She managed to stutter.

"Of course I came darling, but if you don't mind I'd like to go to our room. I'm utterly exhausted."

Sarah put down her wine glass and led Debbie down the hall, carefully closing the door behind her.

"You should have told me you were coming!" She hissed. "I mean I'm delighted to see you, of course I am, it's just... I can't keep being messed about like this. It's not good for us and it's not good for Tom and the kids. I mean, what have you told them?"

"I've left him."

"What?"

"I ended it, I threw him out, told him everything. He went this afternoon and I came straight down to see you."

"But... That... God that's amazing!" She moved forward to take hold of the woman she'd wanted for her own, for so long, but she was brushed away.

"No one can know. Not yet... I still need time to get everything... sorted out."

"Get what sorted out? I mean it's over isn't it? Finished? What is there to sort out?"

"Tom still owns a majority of the business and the house and with us working together... well there are clearly going to be problems."

"In this day and age it's not like anyone can say anything is it?"

"For God's sake Sarah!" her mood could change so quickly. "Isn't this what you wanted? Isn't this what you've been begging for, for months?"

"Yes... yes of course I just—"

"Well then stop bloody complaining!"

"I wasn't complaining I just—"

"Can't you just shut up and be happy? Do you have any idea what I've just given up for you?" She pulled out a cigarette.

"This is a no smoking house..." she said without thinking "But I'm sure Jen won't mind." She added as Debbie lit up anyway.

"I'm ravenous," she said, clearly agitated "ask that woman to cook me something will you?"

"Jen's cooked already. I'll take you out somewhere."

Debbie sighed. "Fine, but I'll have to change."

Sarah just nodded and left the room. She needed a chance to speak to Jen, to somehow explain. She caught her putting away the last of the crockery from dinner.

"I didn't know she was coming." She said, barely above a whisper.

"I know." Jen smiled brightly but continued cleaning.

"I actually thought we might be over, it's just that..."

"That you still love her. I understand of course I do."

"It's a little bit more complicated than that."

Jen stopped and looked up at her, the cheeriness had vanished.

"Sarah... I..."

"Are you coming like that?" Debbie appeared in the doorway looking fabulously glamorous in a red dress. Sarah glanced back at Jen still determinedly cleaning. The two women were so utterly different, the one she'd waited for and the one she wanted.

But she couldn't give up everything she held dear on a whim, a holiday fancy. She looked at Debbie, tall, gorgeous and so commanding, she had wanted this woman for so long and now she had her, she wasn't going to throw this away lightly. She made her decision and strode out of the house with Debbie, leaving Jen to her cleaning.

She didn't see Jen when they got back and in the morning the breakfast was beautifully laid out but Jen was already gone. Debbie complained incessantly about the appalling lack of service and it was all Sarah could do to keep silent.

They spent the day on the beach, Debbie constantly clicking her blackberry, Sarah staring over at the surfers. She was trying to pick out Jen amongst the horde. She thought she caught sight of her a few times, the familiar outfit and graceful movements, but then she was gone again, lost amidst the crowd.

It was a relief to get back to their room and start packing for home. She wanted to forget everything that had happened and stay focused on being happy with Debbie. She stayed in her room. She needed to avoid Jen and she made sure that they aimed for the earliest train so they could be out of the house before Jen was awake. Luckily Debbie was determined to get back into the city for a client meeting, so it didn't take much to usher her out of the door making them a good twenty minutes early for their train.

They dragged their luggage onto the long platform, and Sarah settled on a bench overlooking the beautiful, peaceful beach. It was hot and overhead the palm trees swayed in a whispering breeze; before her the shore lapped serenely against the soft, white sand. She was going to miss the town, with its pretty side streets, its quaint little shops and cafés, its stunning beaches and Jen. She was really going to miss Jen.

She gazed at Debbie, marching up and down the platform trying to compel her blackberry into receiving signal. She thought of London, of the wide windows and bland gray views, of the strangling heat of the tube, of the manic rush of constantly angry people and she thought of Debbie; curt, authoritative, assertive Debbie. She would be with her all day, all evening, all night; Debbie and her blackberry.

She heard the distant train pulling up and suddenly she panicked. She stood, wanting to do something but not sure what.

Debbie strode over to her.

"The quicker we're out of this Godforsaken hole the better." She said, leaning down to grab her bag.

"I can't get on the train." Once the words were out she knew they were true.

Debbie turned to her, confused.

"What do you mean? This is our train."

"I'm not coming back with you." She didn't care if she was doing the right thing. She just knew she couldn't do anything else.

"What do you mean Sarah? We've got to go back. We can't just take an extended holiday! This is so typical of you!" She was shouting over the noise of the train as it eased into the station.

"I can't go back, I can't go back with you. I'm sorry."

"You can't do this Sarah! Do you have any idea what I've lost because of you? Do you? I don't even have a home to go to because of you."

"What do you mean? I thought you threw Tom out" Debbie looked away and the realisation hit "he threw *you* out didn't he?" Sarah almost laughed, so many lies and yet she could still be fooled. "Did he do it because of us, or because he found out about one your little schemes?"

"Look, we'll talk about this on the train." She grabbed hold of Sarah's wrist, but she pulled her arm free.

"I'm not coming with you Debbie." And with that she felt it was over, she knew it was over, she knew she had broken their relationship for good and she was free.

Debbie stared at her for a moment before turning and stepping on the train. She was already back on her blackberry by the time the doors closed and the train heaved itself out of the station, leaving her alone on the platform staring at the beautiful, sun drenched beach.

I Also Met You in Summer

Clare Ashton

Clare Ashton grew up in Wales and lives in Oxfordshire with her partner Jayne and their toddler son Joe. She is the author of Pennance and likes to write fiction featuring strong female characters and more than its fair share of lesbians. She loves to mix suspense, mystery, romance and darker elements too.

You can follow Clare at
http://rclareashton.wordpress.com

THE MOMENT IS STILL so clear to me. I stood outside Angela's terrace house, near Highgate, waiting for the front door to open. Do you remember? She was my new boss at the law firm then.

I saw your slim fingers first, curling round the edge of the door. Your tanned arm, left bare by your vest, was revealed as you pulled the door open. You were looking away, talking to someone in the hall, and took several moments to turn and step into the sunshine.

You looked at me briefly. The sun shone in your eyes, making you wrinkle your nose, and the light made your hair shine white.

'Come in,' you said. 'The barbecue's out the back.'

You carried on talking to a woman in the hall, and I walked through the corridor to the garden.

I watched you all afternoon. You came outside and joined Angela at the barbecue, your backs turned to me. She wore a short dress, and her hair curled down the back of her head and neck. But it was your shoulders where my gaze lingered, admiring your smooth skin, dotted with a few tiny freckles. You put your arm through Angela's and shifted from foot to foot, your slim hips rocking from side to side.

I watched you move around groups of people in the garden; you must have known. You put your arms around someone in every clique, and kissed them before moving on, fleshy lips touching receptive cheeks.

I stayed too long watching you. My skin felt tight across my face from too much sun and I felt dull and tired. I tried to leave quietly, I didn't know many people, and I was closing the front door when your fingers wrapped around the edge and pulled it open again. You looked at me. And I tried not to look at your nipples standing out under your vest.

'You can't be going,' you said. 'I haven't talked to you yet.' You smiled, expecting me to stay.

'Sorry, I'm tired,' I shook my head. 'Thanks for the barbecue.'

I turned to leave, putting my hands in my jeans pockets.

'Shall I walk you to the tube or bus?' you said. I heard the door close behind me, and you joined me without waiting for an answer.

I was confused. 'Won't Angela miss you?'

'Angela?' You frowned and then laughed loudly, bending back, your mouth open wide. 'Oh no, Angela's not my girlfriend.' You laughed again. 'No. Elle's her partner. Although it would be difficult to tell today. She's hiding upstairs out of the sun,' and you rolled your eyes.

I was still feeling stupid from the heat and stared at you.

'Which way?' you said, and you took my hand and walked me out into the street. I wasn't aware of much other than your hand, the soft warm pads of your fingers pressed into mine. I started to sweat down my back, holding myself stiff trying to keep my hand relaxed in yours. I didn't dare move my fingers for the three-mile walk home.

'I like your flat,' you said smiling. We were standing in the living-room bay window that looks over the street and then onto the heath. The road outside was turning orange in the streetlight, and the dark shapes of the trees behind the houses were disappearing into the sky.

'I'd love to live somewhere like this,' you said, looking out of the window. 'Maybe get a dog and walk out on the heath.' You smiled, and turned to look at me.

I sat on the sofa, not knowing what to say. You strolled across the living room and started to look along my bookshelves. You passed the CDs without comment and stopped at the row of books that I hadn't read.

'Oh this is just fantastic,' you said, levering out a book with a finger. You held up the copy of Wolf Hall that I'd won in a competition. You flicked through with your thumb, past the hundreds of pages that I hadn't seen. I nodded as you replaced the book in between Little Dorrit and Underworld.

'Hah!' you said. You turned round, your arms crossed and eyebrows raised. 'What are these then?' You ran your finger along the shelf of colourful paperback romances, and paused before running them down the next shelf, and the next, to the floor.

'Jesus, how many of these do you have?'

I shrugged. 'I don't know. I've never counted.'

You started counting, grinning as the numbers passed fifty and one hundred.

'I've got more upstairs,' I admitted.

You burst out laughing, and clapped your hands together. 'I don't believe you. Show me.'

You grabbed my hand and pulled me towards the door, and took the steps two at a time to the attic. You didn't switch on the light, and you slowed as you entered the room. We could see by the dim orange glow coming through the window in the roof. I stayed half way up the stairs, and watched you through the railings. You didn't look around for my embarrassing books, you seemed to have forgotten, but stared at my desk and chair beneath the window.

'Is this where you work?' you asked.

'When I work from home, or study,' I replied.

You considered the yellow piles of paper on the desk, and slid them aside with your forearm. You sprang from the floor to the chair, and onto the newly cleared space, and didn't pause to ask whether it was all right to open the window. The attic gasped with the noise outside: the sound of footsteps in the street and the growl of traffic in the background.

'You can see the heath from here,' you said in awe. It's dark but I can see people moving on the top. I wonder what they're up to,' you said laughing. You jumped off the desk and turned towards me, your hand outstretched.

'Come up here,' you said.

I climbed the remaining stairs slowly, wondering what you wanted. I stepped closer, but I stopped before touching you. You put your head to the side and smiled, and came forward, sliding your hand around my back. It tickled as you snaked your arm around my side, sending a tremor through me. You pulled me closer, so that I could feel your warmth. Our breasts almost touched and my body tingled with anticipation from my chest, down my belly, between and down my legs. I held my breath, not wanting to lose control with the temptation to pull us together.

'Too fast?' you said.

I snorted, half laughing. 'Perhaps.'

The full moon illuminated your naked body, perfect and pale on my bed. You lay on your back, your arms stretched across both pillows, watching me. The moonlight made you look cool in the warm humid night. I lay on my side next to you, flicking my eyes from your face to your chest. Perspiration burst from my forehead, my armpits, my back.

'You can touch me if you like.' You smiled at me, as I inadvertently licked my lips.

My hand didn't look like my own in the moonlight, all of its heat and colour hidden by the dim light. I felt more confident stretching out unfamiliar fingers to touch your belly, so slowly that I felt your downy hairs bend before feeling your skin. I spread my hand over your stomach trying to take it all in.

I pushed my fingers higher up your body, along the line dividing your chest, and circled my palm around your breast. Your nipple became firm beneath my touch as I gently squeezed it between my thumb and finger. You twitched, and I looked at your face, scared that I had hurt you. But your eyes were large and you still smiled, although your arousal was beginning to take it away.

I knelt up and across your legs, wanting to see you better. I ran my other hand down your belly as I squeezed your breast. You tensed and started to writhe as I touched lower. I ran my fingers over your clipped hair, able to feel the skin, smooth beneath, and where the hair parted, I lingered. It was starting to get wet and I stroked around, teasing you.

Short fast breaths were coming from your mouth, and your smile was gone. You looked at me intensely, as my finger slipped in your moisture. I parted your lips, circling above your clitoris. You gulped and tensed with every caress, and moaned, half sitting up with a spasm, as I stroked firmly across it.

You breathed out with every touch, louder the firmer and quicker I rubbed. Your eyes did not leave mine and your eyebrows creased, your expression pleading with me.

I could smell you, your sweat and moisture mingled, infusing me. My cheeks were flushed and I was dripping between my legs. I started breathing and moaning in time with you as I stroked you quicker and quicker, until your eyes started to close with a look that was almost pained, and your body spasmed, gripped by your orgasm.

You didn't need to touch me, and I fell insatiably in love with you. Do you remember?

It was still summer when you moved in.

I was upstairs in the attic. I'd packed away my trouser suits, which you said made me look too dykey, and was putting my romance novels in boxes under the eaves. I could hear you talking on your mobile downstairs.

'Yes, I'm in. It's brilliant. I can't believe how close this place is to yours. I bet it only takes ten minutes on my bike.'

I guessed you were talking to Angela.

'If you're at a loose end, come round', you continued. 'It's such an amazing place. She's even got access to the garden at the back. I mean the landlady's kids are usually running riot during the day, but it's free in the evenings.'

You went quiet for a while. I stayed still, holding a book over the box. I waited for you to continue, hoping that Angela wouldn't come round. My ears felt strained as I listened to muffled footsteps, and I imagined you pacing around the living room.

'I can't come out now,' you said, sounding irritated. 'I'm in the middle of unpacking.'

You went quiet and I heard the sigh and creak of the sofa, and I supposed you sat down.

'Do you think that's the right thing to do? I mean why now?'

You paused only briefly.

'Yes I can completely understand. I've never known what you've seen in her. But....'

You were quiet again. I carefully put the book in the box, but continued to listen.

'Yes it is crappy timing,' you said, louder and sharper than before.

'No I'm staying here,' more exasperated.

'Yes I do think you should stay with Elle actually. She might be a drippy ginger, fat-arse, but at least she puts up with your shit.'

There was a thud from below, and I imagined you throwing your phone across the living room. The silence gave away my eavesdropping and I shuffled the books in front of me, pretending that I hadn't heard. I was piling in handfuls of books, when your head appeared out of the dark stairwell and into the light by the railings. You held a bar, either side of your head, and peered through with a sad smile on your face.

'You OK?' I asked, putting down the books.

You shook your head. 'Oh it's just another bloody crisis with Angela and Elle.' You looked away for a moment and tutted.

'How about I get you some lunch and a cuppa?' I offered.

You turned back to me with a soft smile. 'I'm going to make you an incredible lunch,' you said, climbing the rest of the stairs. 'I wanted to make the first meal in our home together, and I've got everything for Eggs Benedict downstairs.'

I grinned. Eggs Benedict was one of my favourite foods, but it was you saying 'our home' that made me smile so stupidly. You grabbed my hands and pulled me up, tugging me into an embrace. You squeezed your lips firmly onto mine and spun me from side to side.

'I love you,' you said, holding your face a fraction from mine, and I started to kiss you, so that you wouldn't see the happiness flow from my eyes.

You know that I know this. I wonder if we remember it the same way?

But did you know I came home last summer, on the evening of our anniversary? I wanted to surprise you, a day early after working at a client's site.

I telephoned from the tube station.

'Hey,' you said breathlessly.

'Hi,' I said confused. 'What you up to?'

'I had to run to get my phone. I thought it would be you.'

'Oh,' I said. 'You in the flat?'

'Yes, I was shutting the window upstairs. How's it going? Will you be home OK tomorrow?'

'Definitely,' I said smiling at my deception.

'Can't wait to see you. We'll make up for it tomorrow,' you said, and I could hear that you were smiling.

'Sounds good.' I couldn't stop myself from grinning. 'Can I talk to you properly later? I was just giving you a quick ring.'

'That would be nice. Love you,' and we rang off.

I almost ran the rest of the way. I listened at the door checking that you weren't nearby. My key slid in with the quietest click, and I opened the door and stepped in. I stayed in the hallway, hidden in the shadows, the natural light from the living room and attic not reaching where I stood. I peered around the door into the lounge, expecting you to be sitting on the sofa, reading a book. But you weren't there.

A shuffling sound came from the attic, and the sound of a drawer being shut, and again a drawer quietly closing. A confused snort of a laugh came from my nose, and I frowned as I started to climb the stairs. I held onto the rail, steadying my slow steps, and stretched my neck up to peek through the railings.

Your head came into view first, above where my desk was, and you were facing into the room. I didn't know why you were sitting on my desk, but I recognised your expression. Your eyebrows were crinkled in concentration. You looked down and your mouth had fallen open, short breaths coming from your full red lips. Your naked shoulders and then chest came into view as I stood on the step. I could see your hand clutching at your breast, squeezing it and pinching your own nipple. Your other arm was held straight down between your legs.

I blushed, heat spreading across my cheeks and forehead. The warmth filled my whole body, perspiration breaking on my back. Between my legs pulsed at the familiar sight and sound of you on the verge of coming. Your breathing was getting quicker and your arm moved more vigorously between your legs, out of view. I gulped trying to keep my arousal silent.

I thought I had caught you masturbating, violently pleasuring yourself in my absence. I could feel my clitoris swelling and needing to be touched, pulsing and aching, until, still moving up the stairs, I saw Angela's dark curly hair frothing between your legs.

My heat drained away in an instant. I stared at you both. You gripped her hair in a tight handful, pulling her vigorously into you in time with every squeeze of your chest. Angela slurped between your legs, feasting on you, munching around your lips and then licking up and down. She stuck her tongue in and out of your vagina, making you pant quicker and quicker, and then she closed her lips hungrily around you. She looked like a starving dog with its dinner.

A freezing emptiness started to spread through me. My stomach clenched and I could feel sick sting the back of my throat. I swallowed and gulped trying to keep my nausea and grief down.

Hot tears pooled on my eyes and then ran down my cheeks. I held my breath, not wanting the sobs to escape my mouth. I turned and groped down the stairs in the dimness, flailing for support from the rail and the bare wall. I don't think you saw me. The slurping and panting noises didn't stop, and they followed me down the stairs.

Did I make a noise closing the door? I was starting to lose control by then. You didn't come after me though.

I stayed the night in a hotel, but hardly slept. I phoned in sick in the morning and said that I would work from home.

After you had left, I came back to the flat, slowly opening the front door, afraid of reminders of that scene. There was a half-empty bottle of wine on the coffee table, but only one glass with a sticky red rim. I wandered into the bedroom. The duvet was thrown back from your half of the bed, folded over mine. Had you been considerate, at least not sharing our bed?

I spun around, not knowing what to do. I hadn't slept and my skin seemed to hang heavily from my body from fatigue. I made myself a black coffee and forced myself to climb the stairs to the attic. My legs felt leaden as I stepped up, my desk coming into view again. It was stuffy, and I could smell sweat and sex in the air.

The desk was tidier than I'd left it. My books were in neat piles and my notebooks closed and ordered. The computer screen and keyboard were at the back of the desk, and I pulled them forward to their more usual positions.

I pushed at the window, and it cracked open to the laughter of the landlady's children playing outside. There was the sound of splashing, and I imagined they had their paddling pool out on the lawn. The air outside felt warm on my hands and sunlight bathed my face. My cheeks flushed with the heat, and out of habit I closed my eyes, basking in the warmth.

It was an unbearably beautiful day, but I could take no joy in it. I slumped onto the chair and leant forward, my cheek flat on the desk. I hugged my head with my arms and wept into the surface. Tears ran from the corners of my eyes and pooled wet, sealing my skin against the wood. Body heat and the moisture of my tears resurrected your smell, and your lubrication and a hint of urine filled my nose. I breathed it in, as I shook and juddered sobbing, until I could taste it at the back of my throat. My tears fell more freely still and my cheek slid in the mix of our fluids, mine fresh and yours from the day before.

When you came home, you threw your arms around me. It must have been obvious that I'd been crying, but you looked distraught as well.

'I missed you,' you said, holding me tightly. You wouldn't let go. 'I couldn't reach you on the phone last night. I wanted to talk to you.'

You buried your face into my shoulder and wouldn't look at me. A chill filled me as you clung on, but I didn't push you away.

'Please don't go away again,' you said, sounding like you were about to cry. I thought you knew what I had seen. I thought you full of remorse. You curled up to me that night and I held you, feeling cold and numb.

The acknowledgement of your mistake and my forgiveness went unspoken, but after that, I always chilled at your touch before melting. I no longer overheard your conversations with Angela. You stopped meeting her for drinks and no longer moaned about the undeserving Elle. Angela ignored me at work, but I hardly saw her anyway. She had been promoted and had her own office, away from the open-plan area where I worked.

A new project kept me in the office at lunchtime at the start of this summer. All the desks around me were empty, and a single figure crossing the office caught my eye. I looked up and recognised Angela's bouncing curls, but not quickly enough to lower my gaze in time.

It was less than a second that our eyes met. Did she blush? Had she looked guilty when she looked away, flicking her eyes away from mine, her face tense.

My heart thudded in my chest. I swallowed the fear that started gripping and rising up my chest. I shook my head, to dispel my worries and tried to tell myself that it was only paranoia. But I couldn't concentrate.

In a moment, I twitched and I was on my feet. I walked quickly towards the door. The small pointed heels of my shoes clattered on the stairs, as I rushed down in small restricted steps, my legs bound by my knee-length skirt. I sprinted across the reception, in frustrating half steps, trying to catch Angela. A cushion of warm humid air smothered me when I opened the doors to the street. I was still wearing a jacket, suitable for the air-conditioned office, and broke into a sweat.

I was blinded by the sunshine, reflecting off the concrete and limestone buildings. Buses, taxis and cars screamed past on the road. Shading my eyes, I twisted left and right trying to see Angela. I squinted and bobbed up and down, attempting to see past pedestrians along the street, but I couldn't spot her.

I was about to give up, and I spun around to go back indoors, when your familiar shape caught my eye. Your square shoulders and light hair always stood out in a crowd. You were turning up towards the park, and Angela walked beside you.

I stared after you both, my eyes wide and mouth dropped open. You walked close together and quickly, definitely in a hurry. I expected you to link arms or hold hands, but you both looked nervous and twitched a glance over your shoulder as you disappeared around the corner.

Automatically, I started to run, skipping in and out of office workers. I sped across a lane of traffic, shuffled up the middle of the road, waiting for a gap between cars, and sprinted to the other side of the street. I slowed as I approached the corner, the click of my heels ridiculing my furtive pursuit. I peered around the building. You were at the end of the road, where the grey buildings broke into a slice of leafy green of the park. You were going through the black gates, and I sprinted in small steps along the street, like a crazed clockwork toy, to catch you before you became lost in the park.

The brightness of the pale streets and reflected sunlight gave way to a cool, dark shade beneath the trees. I stopped abruptly, unable to see for a moment with the change of light. I saw someone mirror my movement in the corner of my eye. Up the road, by another entrance, someone else had come to a stop.

I let my eyes adjust, let the glares pulse and fade, and the dark tree trunks, and path mottled with the shadows of leaves, come into saturated view. Sweat had gathered on my forehead and started to run in great drops into my eyes. The person, perhaps twenty metres away, blurred and shifted as I blinked and stared.

It was a woman, quite tall, wearing a dark blue summer dress. The breeze moved the light fabric, flapping around her legs and clinging tight against her hour-glass figure. She was wearing a straw hat with a large rim. Long, red hair hung around her face and deep pink cheeks.

The woman was looking at me. Her mouth was open and her shoulders rose and fell quickly. We stared at each other, both of us heaving for air. I realised my face must have been as red as hers, and I wondered if I looked as comic to her as she did to me.

I was about to awkwardly turn away and pursue you, when I realised who the woman was. She realised at the same time. Her mouth had dropped open with surprise and she slowly raised her hand to her lips. I rocked back on my heels. 'Oh,' I said aloud.

A smile broke behind Elle's hand. I could see her lips turning up and her eyes creasing and shining. She laughed, and shook her head from side to side, still smiling.

I was tempted to say hello, but she turned away and started looking over the park. Reminded of our common pursuit, I turned also, scanning under the trees and across the grass towards the lake. I couldn't see you.

Elle hadn't moved and she frowned. I mouthed 'I'll go this way,' and pointed to the right. She nodded and launched her full figure, flowing in her dress, in the other direction.

I started to run, my heels clicking again on the path. I looked over my shoulder and saw Elle covering the distance more quickly. 'For fuck's sake,' I said, shuffling to a stop. I pulled up my skirt, tucking the rim under my knickers, and kicked off my shoes. I put them under my arm like a rugby ball, before sprinting off around the edge of the park.

I kept looking left, scanning over the park, looking for you, and then back to the path at surprised pedestrians walking in the opposite direction. The grass was busy with children. Students were sprinkled in pairs and crowded in earnest rings. A few older couples had hired deck chairs and were neatly aligned in the direction of the sun, shaded by newspapers.

I'd covered a third of the circuit, when I saw Elle's pink face, undulating bosom and wave of her dress hurtling towards me. We both slowed our run, and jogged, and then walked to meet each other. She raised her palms and shrugged her shoulders, and I shook my head in return.

We sat on the veranda of the café that overlooked the lake. I still had my skirt tucked in my knickers, trying to cool down from our race around the park. Elle's cheeks were beginning to return to a normal colour, and freckles were starting to appear from beneath her flushed skin. She sipped her lemonade through a straw under the shade of her hat, and stared out across the water in front of us. She had long eyelashes that flicked over deep blue eyes, the irises fractured like broken coloured glass.

She turned to me, smiling round her straw. 'You OK?' she said, letting the liquid fall back down into the glass.

I nodded, starting to recover from the exertion. 'Are they definitely seeing each other,' I asked.

'I don't know,' she said. 'All I know is that Angela hasn't tried to touch me for the last six months.

'Six months?' I swallowed and looked away. I tried to remember how many times we'd made love the last six months. Only at weekends I decided, when I'd had a little to drink, to warm me through and stop me freezing at your touch. Was that not enough for you, I wondered.

'I think they've seen each other before though,' Elle continued. 'Angela and I almost split up a year ago. She smelled of someone

when she came home one day. All round her face, in her hair....'
Elle curled her lips up in disgust.

I cleared my throat. 'They definitely had sex about that time. I saw them in the attic....' I looked down into my drink, because my eyes had started to water. I swallowed again trying to continue, but a lump blocked my throat and tears ran down my cheeks.

Elle reached across the table and took my hand. She gently squeezed my fingers. 'Christ,' she said. 'That's horrible.'

I flicked my gaze up and saw her frowning and looking intently at me. 'I thought it was over,' I said, my voice wobbling over the lump in my throat.

She sighed and slowly took her hand away. 'I don't know for sure that they've started again.'

'But you're suspicious enough to follow them around?' I said, smiling at remembering my first glimpse of Elle.

'Yes, I'm afraid so.' She laughed. 'Jesus, what do we look like?' Her hands gestured to her dress covered in sweat, and my skirt that was still scrunched up my thighs. She rolled her eyes and reached over to squeeze my hand again.

'What are you going to do?' I asked.

'I don't know,' she said shaking her head. 'Our relationship's been pretty shitty for the last couple of years. I just wanted to know, for sure, that if was over.' She frowned and sipped her drink.

'Will you try to catch them again?'

'Yes, I need to know now,' she said, serious.

'Do you think that they meet at other times? In the evenings, weekends?' I tried to think of all the times I'd worked late, or seen friends that you didn't like. All of the many opportunities that you'd had.

'Possibly,' Elle said. 'Although I think Angela's extended lunchtimes on Tuesdays and Thursdays are the most likely.'

I shivered when I remembered how you'd told me that you had regular lunch-time meetings a few months ago.

'Seem likely?' she asked.

And I nodded.

'You're not how I imagined,' I said smiling at her. We were strolling back towards the park entrance, under the shade of the trees.

She half turned to look at me, as she walked alongside. She fanned herself with her hat and her hair wafted and pulsed in the breeze. 'How so?' she asked.

'I wasn't expecting someone so, so beautiful,' I said. I looked up at her and saw that she blushed too. But I meant it. She looked like full-bodied, full-lipped Julianne Moore to me.

She frowned and looked forward again. 'Angela hasn't been very complimentary about you I'm afraid.'

I shrugged. 'Oh, I've never been that fussed about her either.'

Elle laughed, and put her arm over my shoulder and squeezed me towards her. 'You have better judgement than me then,' she said laughing.

We'd reached the gate of the park and Elle stopped and turned to me. 'Would you like to have lunch sometime?' She was frowning but was also amused. 'I know it's a bit odd, but it's been nice having someone to talk to about Angela. I won't be offended if you find it too uncomfortable.'

'Yes, I'd like that,' I said. 'And I can let you know if I find out anything.'

'Yes, me too.'

I don't know when things changed. We've been meeting every lunchtime for the past month, and at some point we stopped talking about you.

I took an afternoon off last week and we met by the Serpentine. Elle hired a rowing boat and was waiting for me by the edge of the lake.

'You look nice,' she called out.

I was wearing a straw boater, white shirt and trousers.

'You look just the part,' she said smiling. And I tipped my hat towards her. I was about to tell her how pretty she looked.

'Wait there a second,' she said excitedly, and she reached down into the boat.

'I've brought champagne and strawberries and sandwiches for both of us', she said turned away, 'but, these are just for you.' She turned round with a bunch of flowers. 'For your desk. I thought they'd cheer you up at work. I know what a horrible grey office it is.'

I grinned. She'd bought blue irises, my favourite flowers. I lifted them to my face and the petals licked my nose and the anthers peppered my top lip.

She pointed to my mouth. 'You've got some yellow…' She tilted her head to the side. '…Some pollen, just there,' she said pointing. 'Come here,' she said, giving up, and she stroked her fingers gently across my lips, wiping away the dust.

My lips tingled and seemed to swell where she'd touched, and I looked at her with a content, dozy smile.

'Come on,' she said, grabbing my hand and smiling at me. She led me to the boat, and we both wobbled and swayed as we sat down on the seat. I pushed away from the bank with an oar, and we floated slowly into the middle of the lake.

We only just fitted on the seat across the boat. Our bottoms met in the middle, Elle's ample thighs squeezing warmly into mine. I let my legs relax and fall apart so that our legs touched all the way to our knees.

We stretched out our hands, holding an oar each. As the boat wobbled and became still, our bare arms tickled against each other. I let my arm rest against Elle's, her soft skin making me tingle. I dared not look at her, but she didn't move her arm away. She dropped her oar to rest on the water, and reached out and uncurled my fingers from mine. She stroked them straight and gently held my hand.

I looked ahead, avoiding her eyes. I looked at the beautiful flowers, the champagne and strawberries, at the sun glistening on the water, and at Elle's legs beneath her dress. They all disappeared into a bright flare as my eyes became soaked in tears.

'If we were both single,' I managed to say.

And out of the corner of my eye, I saw her nod, her head hanging down.

Is this too much gushing detail? I wasn't spared any by you. And I know you will still be reading this. You'll be wondering why the flat is empty.

Neither of you were subtle about this weekend. I don't know whether I would have suspected, but Elle confirmed that Angela was spending the same weekend in the same hotel. You were meant to be visiting friends, Angela her brother. It was an opportunity Elle and I couldn't resist.

We've had a busy weekend. Your belongings were packed. If you need them, try the local charity shops. You can buy them back or see your clothes walking around the street on strangers.

That's up to you. You can keep the flat. You've scented every corner and it no longer feels like my home.

Elle and I moved Angela's belongings into her office. You can hardly open her door now. You can see the boxes and suitcases piled to the ceiling through the glass wall. I wondered if it would be too humiliating for her, but Elle didn't think so.

I don't how things will turn out between you and Angela, but I think I do with me and Elle. I met you in summer. I've left you in summer. And I can no longer sign off with love.

Spa Seduction

Kiki Archer

Lesbian author Kiki Archer's debut novel, *'But She Is My Student'* reached number one in both the amazon.co.uk and amazon.com lesbian fiction charts. Thrilled with the novel's success, she has stepped up a gear and aims to have the sequel out by the summer.

Kiki graduated from Leeds with a First Class Degree and spent the following five years teaching in Staffordshire. She has now decided to change career and dedicate her time to writing lesbian novels and fighting the fight for GLBT people.

'KNOBS, THE PAIR OF THEM,' concluded Josie as she grabbed her pink holdall from the conveyor. She had spent the three-hour plane journey moaning and was not quite finished. 'I mean who travels to Russia to watch a football match?'

Anna had heard the argument a million times before and knew it was best to agree. 'I know,' she offered half-heartedly, more interested in her black case that was heading down the ramp and around the first turn; her mother's suggestion of a red tie around its handle now seeming a great idea.

'Little shits, both of them. I mean-'

'She has picked up my case, that lady...' she started to push her way out of the huddle, '...that lady has got my case.'

Josie paused momentarily and then trundled after her best friend, 'I mean ... three days in Venice with us gorgeous girls or a weekend in Russia?' She quickened her pace, 'I still cannot get over it,' the wheels on her pink holdall were really starting to squeak, 'Spa break in Venice with girlfriends or one poxy football match in Russia.' Josie paused for breath, 'Wait up!'

Anna exhaled and tapped the lady apologetically on the shoulder, 'Excuse me I think that is my suitcase.'

The lady lifted up her huge Gucci sunglasses and eyed the black case, 'Looks like mine sorry.'

'Umm, nope I definitely think it is mine,' said Anna smiling awkwardly.

'Let's just have a quick look then.' The lady crouched down and Anna could not help but see her tanned cleavage.

'I just think it shows their lack of commitment to us, how would they-'

'Please just give me a minute Josie, I need to see if this is my...' Anna tailed off as she noticed the lady holding up her best red thong. She crouched down and whispered, 'Yes definitely my bag.'

The lady stared at her chest which was now equally on show, 'I can see that,' she smiled teasingly, 'shame, this would have been a lovely surprise for me at the hotel.' She swivelled the thong on her finger and flicked it back to Anna.

'Sorry,' was all she could manage.

'Don't be, I may get my chance yet,' she said tapping the luggage label, 'I own the spa.'

Anna zipped her belongings back together conscious of the piercing stare.

'Can I offer you a free treatment to apologise for this inconvenience?'

They stood up together, and Anna noted her glowing olive skin and high cheekbones.

'Me too please,' said Josie stretching out her hand. 'Josie Jones, Anna's best friend.'

'Sophia, I own the spa you are staying in.'

Josie was not fazed, 'Has she told you about our saga yet? I mean we must have the worst boyfriends in the world-'

'Ah, now that is where you are going wrong ladies. See you around.'

Anna realised the wink had been for her and started to blush. She watched as Sophia gracefully made her way back to the carousel. 'Can you believe she owns the spa?'

'Yeah she said. She definitely thinks we should dump them and so do I. I mean this has to be the final straw. I am not letting that knob sack of an excuse for a man upset me anymore than he has.'

Anna linked her friends arm and sighed, 'Shall we agree to stop talking about them then?'

'Fine by me,' sung Josie pointing at a sign for the water taxi, 'it is not like I am bothered,' she added.

***

Anna could not believe the magic of it all. The San Clement spa was everything she had imagined and more. Approaching it from the water was incredible. The boat driver had performed a circuit of the island displaying the hotel's standing in all of its glory. Neither were great travellers and they had not been drawn to Venice for the canals, churches or magnificent architecture, instead it was the offer of an all inclusive boutique spa package that won them over. Anna wanted to become cultured, but at twenty two there seemed so much more to be getting on with, and at the moment that priority was a tan. She lifted her face to the warm sun and giggled as some spray splashed against the side of the speeding boat and onto her chest. She thought of Sophia's ample cleavage and smiled at the memory – the first time a woman had ever flirted with her. She was flattered and intrigued. What made someone of such beauty and prestige become attracted to other women?

Josie woke her from her daydream. 'There's Sophia!'

Anna opened her eyes and saw the executive speedboat docking at the wooden platform. She watched Sophia give the driver a double air kiss and could not help but look at her pert bottom as it sashayed from side to side towards the hotel tightly tucked into her white fitted chinos. Her luxury boat reversed and sped away making space for their small, basic vessel. The holidaymakers piled off and headed down the path and into the grand reception.

'OMG! This is incredible.' Josie stood open mouthed.

'I am glad you think so. Please allow me.'

Anna watched as Sophia gave instructions to the smartly dressed bell boys and reached behind the grand desk for a key. The grumbles of the queuing guests became more audible as she instructed the girls to follow her.

Josie nudged Anna, 'Look at us, friends with the owner!'

They walked silently along a wide corridor decorated with floor to ceiling paintings, and then up a wide curving staircase towards the biggest wooden door they had ever seen.

'This is your room ladies. May I?' Sophia opened the door and they both gasped spontaneously. It was breathtaking. To date Anna would have said the Watford Ramada was the plushest hotel she had ever stayed in, but this, this would take some beating.

'I take it you like?'

'It is gorgeous,' whispered Anna, slightly embarrassed that Josie was already lying fully clothed in the humungous bathtub.

'You will fit in here perfectly then,' smiled Sophia reaching for Anna's hand. She lifted it to her warm mouth and kissed it gently. 'If there is anything you need please call me on this number,' she lifted a card from her pocket.

'Thank you,' she said with more confidence than she really felt. Why was her heart beating so fast she wondered?

***

Both girls lay with their heads at the rim of the hot tub, enjoying the warm rays of the sun on their cheeks and the soft tickle of bubbles on their bodies. It had been a blissful morning and Anna felt content. She did not have the same dramatic dilemmas as her friend and was not bothered one bit that her boyfriend had chosen football with mates over fun in the sun, in fact they were barely dating and the time they had spent together had been rather disappointing; always the same with her men - such an anticlimax. She lifted her shades and eyed Sophia making a slow walk around the pool. She was dressed today in tight fitting masseuse whites and her long dark hair was tied tightly in a bun. She was politely handing out leaflets to the relaxing holiday-makers and gifting each one with a personal smile and feeling of importance.

'She has obviously worked her way up then,' declared Josie eyeing the uniform.

'She can work her way up me anytime,' giggled Anna feeling carefree and slightly squiffy from her third pina colada.

'You wouldn't?!'

'I would!'

'You would as well you foxy little bi-curious minx!' Josie lowered her voice as Sophia approached, 'just make sure you give me all of the juicy details.'

'In my dreams, have you seen how hot she is? I am not quite sure I am in her league.'

Josie feigned mock outrage, 'You are one sexy bitch Anna and you know it!'

Sophia knelt down next to the bubbling hot tub and whispered, 'I think you are right Josie, but there is no need to announce it so loudly.'

Josie lowered her white shades, 'Sorry boss, but come on, how hot does she look today?'

Sophia smiled as she eyed Anna's white thong bikini, 'I thought you would like your complementary massage? I am free now if you are ready?'

'Can I go after her?' pleaded Josie suddenly jealous of the attention heaped on her gorgeous best friend.

'I have made arrangements for Ursula to come and collect you in twenty minutes. She can offer you a colonic or a mud wrap.'

'Ursula?'

'Yes Ursula, she is one of our most qualified technicians.'

'Old then?'

'Experienced. Are you ready Anna?' she held out her hand and knew the offer would be taken.

***

Anna lay on the warm leather massage table with her white towel covering her body. She rested her face in the head support and studied the marble floor tiles. Suddenly the lighting dimmed and soft atmospheric music began to play. She lifted her head and smiled as Sophia entered the room and approached the table.

'Any requests?'

'Whatever you are best at.' Anna smiled and returned her head to the cushion. She felt Sophia remove the white towel and heard her feint giggle.

'You did not fancy wearing the pants then?'

This was her first professional massage and she immediately recognised her error. 'I thought it was a shower cap or something.' Anna thought back to the tiny plastic bag that had been resting on top of the folded white towel and began to lift up, 'Give me a second and I will put them on.'

Sophia gently pushed her back down, 'No, I prefer it this way.'

Anna was not sure if it was the freedom of a foreign country or the influence of the potent pina coladas, or her simple desire to just live a little that caused her lack of embarrassment, but she ignored her inhibition and went with it; 'Me too,' she whispered.

The massage was heaven. Sophia was working every inch of her skin, pounding every aching muscle in her body, sending her into a world of pure bliss. Caressed and relieved was the initial feeling, but as the soothing continued she felt a different sort of tension building in her body. Sophia's thumbs were riding up her spine and her fingers were outstretched, gently pulling the muscles on each side of her body. She approached the top of her back and Anna lifted her chest slightly allowing Sophia's reaching fingers to stroke the sides of her breasts. She gasped in desire and eased herself down as the hands returned to the base of her back. This pattern continued with each route up her spine taking an illicit detour ever closer to her hard nipples. She wanted to give a definite signal, a green light that she wanted it, so as the searching fingers returned she lifted herself onto her forearms and arched her back, her breasts now free from the table. Sophia removed her thumbs from the spine and used her nails to slowly drag her fingers to Anna's sides. She teased her desire, edging closer to her nipples, only to return to the centre of her back and begin the agonizing seduction again.

Anna did not know how much more she could take. She needed to feel those fingers, she needed to be squeezed and twisted, she wanted it rough, this delicate touch was too hard to handle. Just as she thought she would scream in despair she felt the hands reach around her pert breasts and scissor her nipples. She was using her fingers to pull and roll and each action caused a groan of satisfaction.

'You like it hard?' purred Sophia.

'Yes, really hard.'

Sophia grabbed both nipples and squeezed them roughly and Anna gasped in delight. She was so aroused and so wet and desperately needed to be pleasured.

'Lift up your ass.'

Anna turned her head and looked deep into Sophia's brown eyes.

'On your hands and knees please.'

The naughtiness in her tone was too hard to ignore so she did as instructed, returning her gaze straight ahead.

Sophia stood at the end of the table and took in the beauty of the firm ass presented directly at face level. She slowly massaged the cheeks, parting them further with each circling of thumbs.

Anna arched her back and opened her legs wider; she wanted it now. 'Do it Sophia, please just do it.'

The power was such a turn on, but her control was starting to falter and the sight of Anna's wet juice slowly sliding down her inner thigh was too much. She buried her face in the moist opening and sucked deeply on Anna's erect bud. Anna screamed in pleasure, quickly begging for more so she continued the deep circling motion with her tongue and used her left thumb to gently ease inside her.

The feeling was one of explosive naughtiness, she wanted Sophia to stick her thumb right in and add her fingers, but she could hardly breathe let alone make demands. It was all so intense, so excruciatingly pleasurable that she tried to hold the tightening, but Sophia sensed it too and sent her mouth into overdrive, literally swallowing Anna's rock hard bud. The spasms shook through her whole body and she wailed her loudest screaming orgasm ever. Sophia kept her mouth in place allowing her to feel every last pulse, every last shudder.

'I think we are done here. Please take as long as you need and make your way back to the pool when you are ready.'

Anna lowered herself onto the table and closed her eyes, feeling the deepest level of satisfaction so had ever experienced. The door clicked closed and she shut her eyes.

***

'So tell me all about it then owners pet!' Josie's ass was still aching from the pipe Ursula had shoved up and the water she had subsequently sprayed in.

Anna slid back into the warm hot tub and thought about where to begin.

Josie peeped over her white shades, 'You look exhausted mate.'

She smiled, 'Yeah I am feeling pretty fucked.'

The Darkness Within

Betty Flack

When she isn't writing, Betty is a University Lecturer, specialising in Education. She lives in the North of England with her partner, wondering what happened to all the socks. Freya Publications will publish Betty's debut novel, *A Changing Girl*, in December 2012.

I HAD BEEN AT THE RESORT only a week, when I first saw the girl. She wandered alone at the water's edge, her ivory skin protected from the sun by the flimsy shade of a parasol. There was something alien about her, as she moved through the shimmering haze and she seemed detached and peculiarly out of place, as if she were searching for something, or someone. I watched her awhile through the grimy glass of the kitchen window, and found myself wondering what she was looking for.

I recall it being particularly hot that day, and by lunchtime the kitchen was almost unbearable. Apparently, even the locals were dying from heatstroke and the chefs complained about it constantly; I could barely blame them, having spent my first week on the island in a kind of sweat-soaked malaise. No wonder the girl was hiding in the shade. With her delicate complexion and flame-coloured hair, she would be ill advised to ever venture out into the sunshine.

"Hey!... *English*!...Hurry up with the garlic!"

I looked around to find Maracio glaring at me from the pass and I quickly returned my attention to the task in hand. "Yes chef," I mumbled, wiping my forehead with a grubby sleeve.

Mother persuaded me that being a chef would open doors. She said I could travel the world whilst still earning a wage. She didn't mention that the job would involve exhausting days in an overcrowded sweatbox, where I could only occasionally view the ocean through the smallest window I had ever seen. Being broiled alive I could scarcely tolerate, but I didn't speak the language either and the isolation was developing into a kind of slow torture, which, honestly, I wasn't sure I could endure. Each day I had a brief respite of 3 hours between lunch and evening service, but otherwise, it was relentless, back-breaking toil and not at all what I'd had in mind when bragging to my friends that I was "*spending the summer in Cyprus*."

As Maracio vented his feverish rage on yet another unfortunate, I returned my attention to the beach, where holiday-makers lay like sundried tomatoes, desiccating before my very eyes in the scorching midday sun. I scanned the shoreline quickly, hoping to catch another glimpse of the pale girl in the flowing white dress, but she was nowhere to be seen.

***

That night I swam in the ocean.

We weren't supposed to. It was against regulations for the staff to mix with the guests and, for kitchen-hands like me, the hotel marina was strictly out of bounds. I didn't much care. In fact, I was secretly hoping to be caught and sacked on the spot, so I could legitimately return to England, blaming my dismissal on social inequalities within the hotel hierarchy. But, at midnight, the beach was deserted and I luxuriated, undisturbed above the black depths of the Aegean. The sea was warm and still from the sun's relentless onslaught and lying on my back, I allowed the current to cradle me as I listened to the rhythmic hiss of surf washing over shingle.

Movement and a flicker of white caught my eye.

And then, from nowhere, the girl was there again. She moved gracefully at the shoreline, gazing out at the water, looking at me, but through me, as if I wasn't there at all.

I swam closer to the shore, wondering at the strange sense of excitement that had gripped me, but I must have drifted further than I had realised, and the current was strong, so far from the beach. Suddenly, I couldn't seem to make any progress and I had a brief moment of panic, as I struggled feebly against the tide. Oblivious to my predicament, the girl continued her journey at the seashore and I stopped a moment and waved, but perhaps she didn't see me, because she continued on her way undeterred, moving further and further away until her elegant figure disappeared into the shadowy undergrowth at the far end of the beach.

Finally freeing myself from the current, I slowly made my way to dry land and dragged myself from the waves, relieved but with the same troubling urgency lingering in my heart. I found myself hurrying across the sand, straining my eyes to find her in the darkness and when finally I reached the place where the beach was separated from the road by a dense hedge of thorny bushes, I didn't hesitate and ploughed blindly into the brushwood, gasping as cruel spikes tore into my skin.

I stumbled from the undergrowth onto a wide, dusty track, which during the day served as a makeshift road leading all the way to the headland. Of course, at that time of night it was abandoned and I stopped a moment, to catch my breath and make sense of my surroundings. It is wild and lonely out there, and even with a full moon hanging like a yellow lantern in the sky, the darkness was practically opaque. Yet again I saw her; she was further along the track, striking out toward the peninsula, her flowing skirt eerily luminous in the moonlight. For reasons I can't quite explain I took after her, although I had no idea why or what I might say if I caught her. Who was she after all; this strange, pale creature, wandering alone in the dead of night? Stumbling along behind her, I watched as she turned off the track, then through a gate to the right, before heading up a rocky trail, which seemed to lead off into the hills. Sometimes now I wonder why it didn't occur to me then to question why she would do that, or for that matter, why I should follow her and, make no mistake, I had every intention of following her. But when I stepped from the road and onto the path, I found it to be littered with great, jagged boulders and was forced to stop. I watched helplessly as she climbed ever higher, feeling quite desolate when eventually she was swallowed up into the darkness. And then, when I could no longer see her, I had an abrupt awakening and gaped down at myself. For I was standing in only my underwear, my cold body dripping and my feet stained with blood.

***

"Hey…English…*concentrate!*" Maracio's rumbling voice stirred me from my musings and I quickly returned to the mundane job of turning the vegetables for midday service. I'd been thinking about the girl again. Suddenly she was all that I could think about, which I know seems rather odd, being as I had only spied her the previous day from a distance and I didn't even know her name. I didn't really know *anything* about her, aside from the fact that she had stolen, like a thief, into my consciousness, and was there all the time behind my eyes; the graceful turn of her head; her pure white skin, like alabaster. And, each time I allowed my mind to linger over her exquisite beauty, I felt almost weak with emptiness, to such an extent that I thought I might cry.

"What's wrong with you today?" Maracio stood over me, his leering face red from the intolerable heat and his barely controlled rage.

"Nothing chef," I mumbled, avoiding eye contact.

I thought he might leave then; this being perhaps the longest exchange we had shared since my arrival to the island, but he remained where he was, watching my trembling hands, as I clumsily worked the paring knife.

He sighed irritably. "Oi!...Stop that!"

I dutifully did and peered upward to find an unusual compassion in his large, dark eyes.

"You not yourself today English..." his tone was uncharacteristically gentle. "What's goin' on? You missing your mama?" I thought the question was sincere and was about to reply that, yes, I was a little homesick, when suddenly he roared with laughter and slapped me hard on the shoulder. Turning to the rest of the kitchen, he shouted something in Greek, which I didn't understand, aside from the word *"mama"* which he spat contemptuously. The kitchen staff laughed in chorus, watching me with obvious derision. Maracio moved his face closer to mine, until the fetid stench of his breath filled my senses. *"English,"* he hissed. "You in ma kitchen now and, girl... you a long way from home!"

***

The light was blinding, when I finally finished my shift and wandered out into the sunshine. It was siesta time, and the holidaymakers lay like walrus around the pool, sleeping off the excesses of lunchtime. I was exhausted and wanted nothing but my own bed, but as I made my way slowly toward the staff quarters, my attention was diverted by a fleeting glimpse of white and I turned just in time to see the girl disappearing from sight, through the far exit of the pool area and into the hotel gardens.

Of course, I followed her and as I crossed into the plantations, where the only sound was the shrill, rhythmic chirrup of the cicada and where the air was thick with the perfume of cyclamen and dog rose, I immediately forgot my previous tiredness and again I was overcome by an urgent need to get close to her. And suddenly it seemed as if I might, for she was only ten metres ahead of me, gliding between the flowerbeds like a wraith. She wore the same white dress as the day before, only today had discarded the parasol, in favour of a silk scarf, which she had draped over her head and shoulders.

"Hey," I shouted. "Wait a moment, will you." But she didn't wait; she simply drifted inexorably forward and even though I was now running, I couldn't seem to catch her. In my inordinate haste, I stumbled and fell to the ground, skinning my knees and palms and by the time I had scrambled back to my feet, I could no longer see her. I raced along the path anyway, toward the perimeter, where a garlanded archway led out to of the hotel grounds. I had never been to this part of the site before and as I crossed the threshold, I was surprised to find myself returned to the same deserted track, from the night before. Sure enough the girl was further along the road with a pale cloud of dust billowing up at her back. It appeared that again she was making her way to the trail and I had no choice but to follow her. I needed to know who she was and where she was going. Why did she walk this way day and night, drifting like a pilgrim in the wilderness?

I called to her then, but my words were caught by a strong tidal wind, and quickly dragged into oblivion.

Just as I knew she would, the girl turned again onto the rocky path, and by day I could see that it wound and twisted all the way to the distant cliffs, where a tiny white chapel, perched precariously above the crashing waves below.

The trail was steep and tortuous, but I moved through the sweltering heat with unfamiliar purpose. Scrambling up the path, I barely noticed the sun beating down on me, or the dust in my nose and mouth. As we climbed ever higher, the landscape became increasingly lifeless, until eventually the arid terrain was only occasionally broken by the hardiest of shrubs and there was no sound above the wind whining across the plain. And still, she climbed higher; like a vision of hope, her outline trembled through the melting haze. I'm not sure how long I pursued her, but when she finally disappeared from sight over the crest of the headland, I felt suddenly parched and exhausted.

Staggering to the end of the path, I stopped, as finally the chapel came into view. The small structure stood on a promontory, facing out at the vast expanse of ocean, which glistened in the sultry heat of the afternoon. As I approached, I saw that the place was derelict and clearly had been for some time. Its only small window was smashed, and the old, sun-bleached door stood broken and slightly ajar. Of the girl however, there was no sign. My heart sank. Had I really journeyed all this way for nothing? Salty sweat dripped from my forehead and into my eyes and as I wandered onto the small terrace, which stood before the chapel door, I stared out at the ocean; alone again. Then a thought struck me and I peered over the cliff edge, at the water hundreds of feet below, which roiled furiously over a few defiant teeth of rock.

The sound of movement disturbed me and I turned, but saw no-one. Still I could hear it; a faint rustling from inside the chapel. Carefully I made my way to the door and peered inside.

The chamber was empty, aside from the girl, who sat on the floor with her back against the wall. She had removed the scarf and now her glorious red hair, tumbled like lava over the flawless, white skin of her shoulders. She peered up at me from the shadows, with obvious surprise.

"It's you!" she whispered.

I stepped inside. "Were you expecting someone else?"

She smiled, a long sad smile, and it was only then that I noticed how plump and perfect her mouth was; and how astonishingly red, her lips. "Yes," she said. "I was."

"Who were you expecting?" I asked, stepping inside, where the air felt cool and clean.

"It doesn't matter. *You're* here now."

She peered at me with her wide, green eyes, which seemed astonishingly bright in the half light and perhaps she knew that she had me then, because there was a sudden alertness about her and she gestured for me to come closer. Like a wretched dog, I crossed the small expanse to sit beside her, trembling slightly with excitement.

"But look at your poor knees," she said, reaching down with fine fingers to delicately trace a line over the broken skin. The sting that accompanied her touch was almost pleasant and I studied her face, drinking in the details of her soft, translucent skin.

"Why do you come here?" I asked gently, but she only smiled and shook her head. Next she reached for my hand, turning it over to examine the raw, grazed flesh. "You poor creature," she said and before I could protest, she was leaning down to kiss my palm, her mouth brushing over the injury with terrible tenderness. She lingered awhile and I realised that I wasn't breathing and I could only sit and listen to the rhythm of my heartbeat, as it drummed so fiercely inside my head.

Carefully, she moved to my wrist, her lips alighting on the tender skin, before following a path up my inner arm to the crook of my elbow. I know I should have stopped her, but at that time, sitting in the darkness, allowing the girl to kiss me felt like the most natural thing in the world; as if I had suddenly found the thing that I was searching for, although I hadn't realised until that moment that anything was missing.

She stopped suddenly and looked up at me with a ferocity that filled me with dread, but then her expression softened and she reached out to touch my face. "So beautiful," she said, before moving in to kiss my throat.

***

It was the daylight that woke me. Brilliant sunshine pierced a crack in the doorframe and blazed into my eyes. The whiteness was blinding and I shielded my face, rolling onto my side. I felt disorientated and a little nauseous; my head was pounding and my mouth and throat felt sticky and dry. It took me a moment to remember where I was, but when finally I did, I struggled upright and peered around me, looking for the girl, but she had gone. I sat against the wall in the tiny chapel feeling acutely alone.

Somehow I managed to stagger to my feet, but standing was difficult and as I gingerly made my way forward, I had to cling to the wall for support. It was getting late, but if I moved quickly I could still get back for the evening service. I pushed through the door and out into the light, where the late afternoon heat was so terrible, I almost crumpled under the weight of it. Still, I had no choice but to get back, and I've no idea how I did it, but summoning every ounce of strength, I lurched down the hillside and back to the hotel.

An hour had passed by the time I finally arrived at the resort, but I barely noticed its passage. I shambled through the evening inferno in a bleary eyed daze, feeling increasingly sick and bewildered. A sea of astonished faces drifted past me and somewhere at the back of my fevered brain I understood that I must be an appalling sight. My skin was burning and the sweat was running off me in thick rivulets. I think it was around this time that I first noticed the feeling; a hollow, gnawing sensation deep inside me; not quite hunger, and not quite thirst- but rather a kind of *yearning*, although at that time, I didn't understand the object of it. I only knew it had something to do with the girl and what had passed between us.

When finally I arrived at the kitchen, I was met at the door by Maracio. Such was his rage when he first saw me, he didn't comment on my pitiful state. Instead, he bawled me out, ranting about where I had been and demanding to know what the hell I was doing, not turning up for work. This only compounded my confusion and I stood looking at him, not knowing what to say. I was only a few minutes late after all and I hadn't missed a single day of work, since arriving in Cyprus. What in God's name was he talking about?

Perhaps sensing my confusion, he paused and it was only then that he seemed to actually see me. His anger was instantly replaced with genuine concern, which I remember rather frightened me at the time. Whatever must I look like, to engender such a response from him, of all people?

"Louisa? Are you alright? What has happened to you?"

I couldn't speak, but shook my head and stood looking at him dumbly, suddenly feeling that I might cry.

"Where have you been? You've been missing for two days? I was about to call the police?"

Two days? But surely I'd only been gone a few hours. It was all too much, and I think I must have fainted then, because the next thing I remember was lying on the wet, kitchen tiles, only vaguely aware of Maracio talking above me. His voice sounded distant and distorted.

"Sun stroke...Lying out in the sun...So thin...Look at her skin... Doctor....Get a doctor!"

*

The days that followed are lost to me now. I retreated to the shade of my lodgings and at some point a doctor did come to see me, but she could find nothing wrong. The strange burning of my skin healed quickly and, so long as I stayed out of the sun, I felt no pain. There was only the feeling that remained; twisting and growing inside me, like a darkness spreading out of control; an ink blot seeping outward, filling each and every cell with its permanent stain.

Maracio and the Hotel Manager came to see me once, but they stood at the far end of my bedroom, watching me in my shadowy tomb, as if they were slightly afraid of me; or perhaps of what I was becoming.

"I'll come and see you tomorrow," Maracio called as he shuffled quickly out of the door, but he didn't. Nobody came the next day, or the day after that and I lay alone, writhing in the darkness, willing the feeling to leave me; and wondering whatever Maracio had meant, when he whispered *"Lamiae"* to his companion, as they hastily made their exit.

I don't know how much time had passed, when I first struck upon the idea that *she* might be able to alleviate my suffering, but I know it was at night. And then of course, it seemed obvious, because when I held an image of the girl in my mind, the feeling lessened a little; how much more so if I actually could see her, be with her; perhaps even hold her? So, like a ghost, I rose from my bed and wrapping my sheets about me, I wandered in a daze to find her.

She wasn't on the beach, although I walked for hours by the water's edge. Nor was she anywhere in the grounds of the hotel, because I searched and searched. Finally I had no choice but to journey back to that place where it happened, the small temple on the cliff edge and somehow, as I climbed the treacherous path again, it didn't seem quite so difficult and I felt renewed by the moonlight, the cool night air and the promise of seeing her; for surely she would be here, perhaps even waiting for me to return. But, just as I had left it, the chapel was deserted. I wandered inside and, feeling a little reassured, I lay down in the darkness, waiting for her to come back.

***

Still I wait.

Sometimes I venture out, roaming the land and searching; *always searching.*

She isn't here, although sometimes others come; curious witnesses to my nightly passage, who eagerly follow me to this lonely spot. Their company refreshes me for a while, but after they depart, like shadows before the dawn, the feeling quickly returns, never to leave, always to remind me of the girl who brought me here, to this place; to this end.

***

Signals

Sam Paterson-Sleep

Sam Paterson-Sleep is a part-time Performing Arts tutor and sporadic writer. She is an avid women's football supporter, spending much of her free time travelling the world following England Women and blogging her adventures for an online women's football magazine. Her teaching and travels allow her to observe all manner of folk, who, in turn, inspire and enrich the characters in her stories. She set up home numerous years ago with her partner and cats in Sussex.

A BEAD OF CONDENSATION trickles its way down a glass. She pushes her change into her pocket, picks up the glasses and turns to face the crowds. The dance floor is tightly packed with bodies writhing to the music. She worms her way from the bar. Voices shout orders behind her, repeating them louder to be heard over the music. Hands pass drinks back to dancers who have paused for a moment to talk, to look, to touch.

Three drinks, balanced unevenly in her hands. She slowly works her way through the crowds, jostled by the bodies dancing, pulsing to the beat. The bass reverberates through her chest. She side steps a dancer, making eye contact as she passes. A smile whispers at the corner of her mouth. She looks down at the drinks rocking in their glasses, breaking the moment. An arm jerks unexpectedly by her, making sharp contact with her arm, the drinks slosh over the top of the glasses. Dark liquid flows over the rim, onto her fingers, and drips onto the floor. She apologises, an automatic reaction. A dancer, oblivious to her presence, lost to the rhythm of the music, moves in front of her, invading her space, nudging the glasses closer to her, tempting the dark liquid to overflow for a second time. She pauses, closes her eyes and waits for her way to clear, for the dark liquid to settle. She breathes in and opens her eyes. She looks around, catching sight of them across the dance floor. From here she can't see them clearly enough to read their body language. She looks away, focusing on her immediate surroundings and moves away from the crowd at the bar.

She reaches the edge of the dance floor, writhing with bodies, hot from dancing, pulsating to the music. She looks over at them, she is closer now. Their body language is animated, yet hushed. There seems to be an urgency to their conversation. They lean closer to hear each other over the music, their bodies remaining apart. A hand touches an arm, quickly shrugged away. She looks back at the dance floor, edging forward to avoid the dancers moving in time to the music, lost in their own world of pleasure, unaware of her as she moves past them. She looks again. The hand returns to the arm, allowed to rest there for longer this time, before the arm gently moves away. The hand returns, this time closing around the arm, gently pulling the arm closer. They lean closer, but still their bodies remain apart. She can't tell what they are talking about, their body language is ambiguous. She knows tension can rise all too quickly between them; she has seen it happen before. It would start with a badly-phrased comment, then a quip, a curt response. Slowly the temperature between them would rise, body language becoming stiffer, then more fluid, exaggerated, as the tension built. She sighs, hoping for calm this time; hoping for a smile, a signal that all is well. The bass line changes, more urgent this time as the music swells the tempo rising. The hair on the back of her neck responds, rising, a subconscious reaction to the shift. The bodies around her move closer, almost daring each other to make that first contact, to break through the invisible wall standing between them and the intimacy the music is beginning to demand.

A bead of condensation trickles down a glass. She looks at her drinks again, she can feel the spilt drink on her fingers. It feels sticky and sweet on her skin. She looks at them again, she is closer still. Their body language remains confusing; they are closer yet still apart. They exchange brief touches, they seem awkward to her, stilted, stiff almost. They seem unaware of the change in the music, unaware of it throbbing through the room, unaware of the bodies closing round them, pressing into their backs, unaware that she is watching them, searching for some clue. Is she to walk back to a repeat of last time? Then she had stumbled back to them, three drinks balanced unevenly in her hands. She hadn't paid attention to their body language, to those silent signals that would have warned her of the tension. She hadn't paid attention. She hadn't seen. She had felt the tension when she gave them their drinks, heard the uncomfortable silence, seen the awkward smiles. By then it had been too late to make an unnoticed retreat. She had tried to make light of the situation then, to lift the mood. Everything she had tried had fallen on deaf ears, uninterested participants gazing out across the dance floor. A night disturbed, affected by her not paying attention. This time she would see, she would pay attention. She watches them as she winds her way closer, through the hot bodies pulsing to the music.

The hand moves up the arm onto the shoulder, pulling closer. Words, unheard to her, whisper into an ear. They pause, and then look around. Eyes dart through the crowds, looking, searching. Her face breaks into a smile; she raises the glasses in acknowledgement of the searching look. A dancer, unaware of her attempt to make contact, moves in. She sees the dancer's lips move, the words stolen by the music. She smiles half-heartedly in return, her eyes trying to indicate she is going somewhere else, to someone else. The dancer moves closer, eyes examine her, mentally undress her, eager to reach out, to touch. She smiles again, apologetically this time, raising her eyebrows briefly before finding a way round, a way past this unexpected intimate attention. The dancer turns, a predatory smile forming, watching her work her way through the crowd.

A bead of condensation trickles down a glass, pausing at the crook of her fingers, as if waiting for another before it continues down. The bass courses through her, vibrates through her chest as if trying to force her heart to beat to the same urgent rhythm. The hand still rests on the shoulder, heads now angled in towards one another. Words unheard spoken between the two. Eyes no longer searching the dance floor, their focus no longer shared with others, now looking only at each other. She is unseen by those she wants to be seen by, those who she wants to either welcome her in or warn her away. She is seen by other eyes, eyes that want more of her than a brief dance floor encounter, more than a fleeting smile.

She has seen this before, an almost memory suggests itself briefly. A thought just out of her reach tempts her into thinking. She has seen this before.

The hand shifts as if searching for a more comfortable resting place. Fingertips brush the skin of a neck before being shrugged away. The eyes glance round the room again, searching. She reads the signals as eager, urgent. She starts to react to this new search, a smile almost forms, glasses briefly jerk up. The drinks slosh, dark liquid spills out of a glass, unnoticed. It trickles over her fingers, drips onto her shoes and down to the floor. She stops herself, suddenly unsure if she has read the signals correctly. She has seen this before. The ghost of memory teases her. A thought, tantalisingly close. She has seen this before. Her head twitches briefly, almost a shake as if to dislodge the thought. She frowns and pauses. She looks again, this time more careful to understand what she sees. A bead of condensation trickles down a glass to join the other in the crook of her fingers, waiting. Their body language tenses, stiffening with anticipation. Eyes searching, try to find her, unclear in their message. She can't interpret the signals, doesn't understand what she is seeing. A hand hesitantly reaches out. The gentlest of touches on a cheek, turning the head back to look only at the eyes. Faces move closer, lean in slowly. She knows she has seen this before. She waits, anticipating their next move, she understands the signals now. Reads the message of their body language. Knows now what was to come. Faces so close, almost touching. Without realising she holds her breath. She doesn't notice the music change, the bodies around her slow to a more sensual movement, moving closer to each other, reaching out to make that longed-for contact. Fingers touch, slide gently, carefully, upwards over skin made hot by the closeness, caressing, teasing round the edges of clothing, gradually making their way to the nape of the neck. A hand hesitantly reaches for a hip, feeling the denim, finding the waistband & following it slowly round to the small of the back. Faces growing ever closer. She keeps watching, transfixed by it all, anticipating the next move, not believing it will happen. Her heart pounds, her breathing is shallow. Bodies around her writhe slowly, intimately, in time to the music. A bead of condensation trickles down a glass, reaches the crook, overflows down her fingers, splashing on the floor as it falls. She stands there, almost frozen, suddenly aware of her heart pounding against her chest, unable to tear her eyes away. The music throbs, vibrating through her, dictating the movement of the bodies around her, her breathing now deep and jerky. Their lips meet. A kiss. She didn't believe it would happen. A kiss.

The confused body language, the signals she couldn't interpret. She should have understood. She should have known. But she hadn't believed it would go that far. Secrets had been kept from her, conversations whispered when she wasn't listening, telling looks exchanged when she wasn't watching. Her breath caught in her throat. A long, deep kiss. Their bodies move closer, limbs intertwine; they were oblivious of everything surrounding them, aware only of each other. A ghost of thought comes so close to touching distance.

A bead of condensation trickles down a glass and over her fingers. The bass line shifts, bodies break apart from each other, caught up in the hysteria of the music, more tribal now, ritualistic, finding some kind of catharsis in the music, losing themselves to the freedom of the dance. A body twists into her. Her arms move suddenly without her control. The glasses jerk. Dark liquid swirls, tumbles up and out, splattering her top. The liquid soaks quickly through to her skin. The unexpected cold waking her from her thoughts, making her cry out and glare around her, unaware of which body was responsible. She looks back at them. They are still locked together in their private intimacy. She moves towards them, hesitant in her actions; her heart beating clearly in her ears. She carefully rests the glasses on a nearby table, finally releasing her grip on them. She pulls at her top, separating it from her hot sticky skin and wipes her hands on her jeans. She looks at them again, picks up one of the glasses and takes a sip. She looks back at the dance floor. She sees someone looking at her, watching her, with a predatory smile. She holds the eye contact, raises an eyebrow slightly; the corners of her mouth slowly start to curl up into a smile. The bass pulses through her body, and slowly she allow it to take possession. She glances at the two new-found lovers she came with. She looks again at the predatory smile; into the eyes of the dancer. She drains her glass, places it back on the table and slowly licks her lips. She feels the music vibrating through her and slowly moves her way back across the dance floor. Back to the predatory smile. Back to the dancer.

***

One Weekend

Franki Morgan

Franki lives in South East Spain with her two nutty dogs. When she's not spending too much time on the computer she can be seen out hiking with the dogs and taking photographs.

"IT'S SO UNFAIR. Everyone else gets to go away for the weekend and I get stuck at work; all because the boss wouldn't let me swap my shift," I muttered under my breath, as I stood behind the reception desk at the hotel where I worked. "A Friday night and I'm stuck here at work while everyone is on holiday."

"I'm sorry to disturb you, but I was wondering if you had any rooms free?" a woman's voice said.

I looked up from my mutterings to stare at the greenest eyes I'd ever seen. I felt myself getting drawn into the eyes and couldn't pull myself back. I forgot what the voice had asked.

"Erm, is everything alright?" the voice asked.

"Oh I'm sorry," I said kicking myself for staring. "I was a bit distracted. What did you ask?"

"I was wondering if you had any rooms available. I was due to be staying with my sister and her husband, but they've both come down with a bug and the doctor has advised that I don't stay with them, so I need a room for a weekend please."

I looked down at the computer screen to see what rooms we had free. "I've got a room here that has a little terrace that overlooks the park to the back of the hotel."

"That sounds perfect thank you. Here are my passport and credit card for you."

I looked at the passport, as I took a copy of it for our records. How could anyone look so pretty in her passport photo? *My* passport photo looks like a criminal's mug shot, principally due to my blonde hair being very short and spiky at the time of the photo being taken. I'd let my hair grow out a bit since then so I didn't have the spikes anymore – in fact I could have done with a haircut as it was starting to flop into my eyes. I filled in all the registration information on the computer and handed back the documents.

"I'll just get the key for your room and take you up there, Miss Jameson."

"Thank you. You can call me Ali. I can't wait to get up to the room and kick my shoes off. I was stuck in a meeting all day, organising a move down to this area to be closer to my sister and her family and now I just want to relax for a little while."

I picked up the room key and walked from behind the reception desk, reaching down to collect Ali's suitcase.

"If you'd like to follow me I'll take you up to your room then."

"Is there somewhere to get something to eat near here? She asked. "My sister was supposed to be cooking me a meal, but with her being ill it's not going to happen and I'm getting hungry."

"If you're happy with pub food then there is a nice pub just around the corner. They have nice freshly made food and it's a decent price as well."

"That's great thanks. I think I'd better freshen up and then go out before I sit down; otherwise I don't think I'll move again tonight."

We arrived at the room and I got the key out and opened the door, signaling to Ali that she should enter the room first. She brushed up against me as she walked through the door and I felt my body stirring. I stood in the doorway watching as Ali strolled around the room checking it out. I guessed that she'd come straight from work, as she looked very smart in a tailored jacket and skirt. As she reached into the wardrobe to get a coat hanger, her shirt stretched tightly across her chest. I felt my mouth go dry as I watched her and decided to leave the room before she caught me staring.

"I'm going to put your case on the side here and then leave you to get yourself settled in."

"Thanks. I don't want to leave it too long to go and get some food or the kitchen will be closed at the pub."

Our hands brushed as I handed over the key and I felt the electricity pass between us. I quickly turned and left the room, closing the door behind me before I made a fool of myself. I made my way back to the reception desk, imagining all the fun I could have been having, if I'd been able to go away with my friends this weekend. It wasn't fair - I was only working tonight and then I was off for the weekend, so if my boss had been nice and let me have tonight off, then I could have gone. The only highlight so far had been booking Ali into her room.

I was tidying up behind the reception desk, when I saw Ali again; she was on her way out. "Enjoy your meal." I called out as she walked past me.

"Hopefully I will. I'll see you later." She said to me as she walked out of the front door.

I watched her leaving the building, amazed at the difference in her. She was no longer the tough looking woman in a business suit - Ali was now wearing form fitting jeans and a shirt. She'd also let her hair down and the dark curls were bouncing around her shoulders as she walked. My eyes worked their way down her long legs as she walked out of the hotel doors. "Now that is the way that jeans should fit a woman," I thought to myself, before shaking my head to clear my thoughts and get on with the tidying up.

The next morning I was lying in bed contemplating getting up, but really not wanting to, when the dog jumped up on the bed to let me know it was time to get up. "Ok I'm getting up. Leave me alone!" I complained. I wasn't sure what I was going to do for the day. It was supposed to be a nice day so maybe I'd take a picnic and walk the dog over by the lake and let her play in the water, whilst I relaxed on the shore. I'd bought a new book the previous day that I had been trying to read, but something kept getting in the way, so now was a perfect time to read it. I ruffled the fur on Scruff as she lay next to me on the bed.

"What do you think about that then Scruff? Do you fancy playing in the lake today? We can take a picnic with us and have a hike up there and maybe you can run off some of your energy!" Getting dressed in my shorts, t-shirt and with my sports bikini on underneath, I walked downstairs to get the picnic ready. A short while later I had everything packed up in my rucksack, and I grabbed Scruff's lead, along with the car keys. "You ready to go then Scruff?" I asked, looking at Scruff who was jumping up and down by my side, getting excited because she knew we were going on a walk.

"Come on then. Let's go." I opened the door and walked to the car. I put my rucksack into the boot of the car and then opened the back door so Scruff could jump in. I got into the car and headed off towards the lake. As we got closer to the car park Scruff started getting excited as she recognised where we were heading. I pulled into a space and opened the back door to let Scruff out. She started running around in a circle, excitedly. "Hang on girl!"

I looked around the car park and was pleased that there didn't seem to be many other cars there. Hopefully that meant that it would be quiet on the trail and by the lake. It was always nicer here when it was quiet. I started off up the trail while Scruff ran on ahead and then ran back to me to make sure I was following her. Eventually we reached the lake and Scruff ran and jumped straight into the water.

"You are so daft, dog!" I called out to her. Walking over to the water's edge, I laid my blanket under one of the trees. This would be a perfect place to sit and relax. I could see Scruff in the water, but I would also be safe from the heat of the sun later on. I took my shorts and t-shirt off and got my book out to start reading. Thirty minutes later, hunger forced me to relinquish the book and reach for the sandwiches. As I was eating, I looked around the lake to see how many other people were near us, but it was very quiet. I was surprised that there were so few people enjoying the water today. Normally by this time there would be a few families around with children playing in the lake. I spotted a few people in the distance, walking along the trail, but they didn't seem to be interested in stopping by the lake. *That's good*, I thought. I much preferred to have peace and quiet while I sat here. After I finished my lunch I picked my book back up and started to read again. Scruff decided she wanted to go back in the water so she ran off to play again. I looked up when I heard a woman squeal loudly and saw Scruff shaking her wet coat all over a hiker. "Uh oh!" I thought, as I jumped up to go and grab her.

"I'm so sorry about her", I called out as I ran over to the woman. "Scruff, come here, you bad dog." I grabbed hold of Scruff's collar and put her lead back on her, as I told her off for getting the lady wet. I turned to face the lady ready to apologise to her again when I realised I was looking into those amazing green eyes that I recognised.

"Ali! What are you doing out here?" I asked.

I saw Ali's eyes stare at my bikini top before they flicked up to look at my eyes. "I fancied getting out of the hotel for a while and I was looking at the leaflets in the room. It mentioned this hiking trail and lake. I thought it would be nice to get some fresh air. I don't get the chance to spend time outside when I'm at home working. I just didn't expect to be accosted by a dog when I got here!"

"Scruff didn't mean to upset you..." I started to say before I realised that Ali was joking. "Would you like to sit over with me on my blanket and I'll protect you from the horrible dog?" I laughed.

"Oh an offer I can't refuse," Ali said as we started back to my blanket, with Scruff running back into the water.

We sat on the blanket for the rest of the afternoon chatting as though we'd known each other for years. When we got too hot in the sun we stripped off our shorts and went into the lake to cool off. Ali looked amazing in her bikini, with legs that seemed to go on for miles and I struggled not to stare at her when we went into the lake. I could feel her eyes on me too throughout the day, but she looked away every time I caught her staring.

"I'm going for another dip too cool off." I said standing up and extending a hand to help her. "You coming?"

"Sounds like a good idea to me," Ali said, grabbing my hand to pull herself up. She didn't let go of my hand as she started to walk towards the water so I left my hand in hers. It felt nice to be walking hand in hand with her and I again I felt my body stirring. We started to walk into the water when Scruff ran past Ali and bumped into her. She began to fall, but I caught her around the waist and pulled her against me. Her body felt nice against my own, we seemed to fit together perfectly.

"My hero!" Ali joked as she held onto me. "You saved me, so how should I repay you?" She asked.

"Hmmmm, let me think about that. What would I really enjoy?" I asked as I stared into her eyes and started to lean towards her.

Ali slowly moved forward a fraction and kissed my cheek. "How was that?" she asked.

"Not a bad start, but I'm sure that saving you deserves a bit more than that." I said.

"How about this?" Ali said as she kissed the edge of my mouth.

"That's getting better, but I still think I deserve more."

"And this?" as she kissed my lips slowly.

I leaned into the kiss and opened my mouth to allow her tongue entry. I moaned as she carried on kissing me.

"How was that?" Ali said, once she'd pulled her mouth away from mine.

"I think we're getting very close to payment." I said as I winked at her. "Maybe we should try it a few more times just to check."

Ali ran a hand through my short hair and pulled my head towards her so our lips met. "I think that sounds like a great idea." She said and she kissed me again.

I have no idea how long we stood there kissing, but eventually Scruff came over and nudged her way between the two of us forcing us apart.

"Wow!" I said as I took some deep breaths. "I like your method of payment. I should save you more often."

"I would like that." Ali said with a grin on her face. She rested her arms on my shoulders and held me close.

"What do you have planned for the rest of the evening?" I asked her.

"I hadn't thought about it really. Probably go and get some dinner somewhere and then go back to the hotel."

"I was going to get a Chinese takeaway and then watch a movie. Would you like to join me? You could follow me back to my place and have a shower and change if you want. I've got some spare clothes you can borrow."

"I would love that. What movie do you fancy watching then?"

"Oh I've got plenty of movies. We'll go back to my place and see what takes our fancy." I held my hand out to Ali and we walked back to the blanket to collect the remains of the picnic and all the other bits and pieces. We walked back to the cars and then Ali followed me home. I kept looking in the rear view mirror to make sure she was still following me and hadn't changed her mind and gone back to the hotel. I pulled up outside my house and Ali pulled in behind me. We got out of the cars and went into the house.

"Make yourself at home. I'll show you where the spare bedroom is and the bathroom and you can have a shower and get changed. I've only got the one bathroom so if you have your shower first I'll have one after you. Then I'll meet you down here and we'll order some dinner."

"Lead the way then."

We walked upstairs and I pointed out where the bathroom was. "My bedroom is here and the spare bedroom is right next door," I said opening the doors to the two rooms. "I'll leave you here to get your shower and I'll put some clothes on the bed in the spare room for you."

I walked into my bedroom to find some spare clothes for Ali. I could hear the water from the shower and started to imagine Ali naked in there. I walked away from the bathroom before Ali came out and caught me standing there. The bathroom door opened and Ali walked out with a towel wrapped around her and tucked in between her breasts. I gulped as she walked past and brushed up against me and she smirked as she walked into the spare room, closing the door behind her. I grabbed my towel and hurried into the bathroom. Stripping off, I started the shower and climbed in. I closed my eyes as I put my head under the stream of water, trying in vain to clear my mind of the image of her as she walked out of the bathroom. Before I knew what was happening the shower curtain was pulled back and Ali joined me in the shower.

"You really should lock your door if you don't want a visitor while you're in the shower," she said as her hands worked their way around the front of my body and up to my breasts. "I thought of you all alone here in the shower and decided it would be a waste if I didn't join you." Her hands started moving down my body and my legs started to tremble. I leaned back into her and let her hands continue their investigation of my body. Before I knew it her fingers had slipped between my wet folds and I was climaxing around her fingers. I couldn't remember a time that I had been so turned on and come so quickly.

"Wow, you can join me in the shower at anytime you want to!" I said as my breathing slowed down. I turned around in Ali's arms and kissed her. "How about we take this to my room. I think it's my turn with you this time."

Ali reached around me and turned off the shower, then took my hand and led me into the bedroom. Pulling back the covers I climbed in and lay down. Ali climbed on top of me. I groaned as I felt her body on mine. It felt so right. She leaned down and kissed me, her hands roaming all over my body.

I rolled Ali over so I was on top of her. "I said it was my turn." Leaning down, I kissed her, whilst my hands moved their way down her body. My fingers slipped easily inside her; she was so wet for me and, as my fingers moved inside her, she moaned. Her body moved in time with me, but before she could climax, I withdrew and moved my hands to paint Ali's breasts with her own wetness. I lowered my head down to kiss her breasts clean and to taste of her, before moving my hand back down Ali's side to reach the curve of her hip.

"Please...." Ali pleaded.

I slid my hand teasingly over towards her mound as I moved back up her body to kiss her lips. "Please what?" I said between kisses.

"I need you back inside me.... I need to come." Ali whimpered.

I skimmed my fingers lightly over her and she groaned again.

"I'm so close, please don't tease me."

I moved my fingers back inside her, but this time I held them still. She started to move against my hand but I still didn't move them. "Come on Honey, you can do it." I said to her.

I could feel her getting close to climaxing and, just as she was about to come I started to move my fingers. She climaxed and I moved my fingers more quickly. I felt her muscles tightening around my hand as she climaxed a second time.

"Wow!" She said, struggling to breathe. "I think I just died and went to heaven! That was amazing."

I rolled onto my back and pulled her into my arms allowing her to curl her body around mine. Her heartbeat returned to normal, as I slowly kissed her. I thought she'd gone to sleep when she said in a sleepy voice. "You know, I love the blue of your eyes. They are so soulful. I feel you can see right inside me."

I lay still, watching her fall asleep, thinking how perfect it felt to have her in my arms. I should really thank my boss for not allowing me to have yesterday off! I drifted off to sleep wondering how the day had turned out to be so different from what I had expected.

The tingling of my body woke me up a while later as I felt Ali kissing her way down my body. Slowly, I opened my eyes and looked down to see Ali watching me as she kissed my breasts.

"You've decided to wake up and join in the fun have you?" She asked.

"I thought you were tired," I said.

"I was for a while, but then I got this urge to taste you and I couldn't wait for you to wake up so I decided to make a start." She moved lower and I felt her open my thighs then she had her mouth on me.

My breath caught as she feasted on me. I could feel my body tightening as my climax was building and before I knew it I felt myself explode as my climax hit me. "Oh wow. I've never come so hard in my life." I said.

Ali rested her head on my stomach as our breathing slowed down. "I enjoyed that." She said as she gazed back up me.

"Come back up here" I said, and I held my arm up for her to curl into. I kissed the top of her head as she settled down with her head on my shoulder, her arm lying across my stomach. "What plans do you have for the rest of the weekend?" I asked.

"I've lots of plans." she replied.

I felt my euphoria drop. "Oh ok. That's fine then."

Ali lifted her head to look at me. She put her hand on my cheek to move my face round to face her and kissed me before saying, "My plans mostly consist of having my wicked way with you in the kitchen, the sitting room, the bathroom again and many more times in the bedroom." I felt myself drowning in her eyes before I realised that I'd missed what she'd said to me.

"What did you say?"

Ali repeated herself, with deliberate slowness.

I must have had a gleam in my eye when I said, "So you really don't have any reason to leave the house for the rest of the weekend... I think I like your plans."

***

"The Sighing Sound, The Lights Around the Shore."

Toni James

Toni James was born in London, but later moved with her family to Lancashire, where she remains. For more than ten years she taught English in schools across the region, before taking up an advisory role. She is a prolific writer of poetry, short stories, plays and novels. Her work has been published both in Europe and the US. *The Sighing Sound, the Lights Around the Shore,* was first published in a collection by Alyson Publications in 2007.

THE MOMENT I SAW HER, I knew.

She walked into the bar and there was a sudden lightness in my soul. With casual grace she crossed to the table and stood before me, her smile quizzical, her gaze penetrating. We looked at one another for some time without speaking. There was a glimmer of recognition in my mind; although this was our first meeting, I felt I had known her before. As she regarded me, the corners of her mouth betrayed the beginning of a smile and suddenly I found it difficult to breathe.

Finally she spoke. "Do you mind if I sit?"

"Not at all," I replied.

She relaxed in the chair opposite and I took a moment to study her. She had a lean, muscular frame and the alert posture of an athlete. Her smooth skin seemed to glisten in the moonlight and contrasted sharply with the pristine white of her shirt. She wore her dark hair very short and it fell naturally into a pleasing array of curls. Her handsome face was almost feline, with high cheekbones and a delicate mouth. And her hazel eyes were rich and inviting, like warm caramel.

I was transfixed.

She returned my gaze with a self-assurance that was challenging, but at the same time, exciting.

"Have you been waiting a long time?" she asked finally.

I couldn't help smiling. "You arrived just in time."

She was suddenly serious. "Is there somewhere you would like to go; something you would like to do?"

I considered the question. All at once, a thousand thoughts collided in my mind and I blushed. "Maybe a walk," I ventured.

She stood immediately and offered me a hand.

Hesitating before taking it, I breathed in deeply. It seemed a significant moment and I wanted to be sure I was paying attention. Finally I summoned the courage and placed my hand in hers. Her skin was soft and warm and as her fingers closed around my own, I felt an unfamiliar surge of elation. My legs felt strange as I climbed to my feet and my heart raced painfully.

She guided me out of the bar and to the street. Tourists passed in a blur as we headed from the bright, main strip and away to the darker streets beyond.

When completely alone, she turned to face me. "Where shall we go?" She was flushed and a light sheen of perspiration had broken out on her brow. Although late, the evening was hot and humid. Before I could stop myself, I reached out and stroked her face, moved momentarily by her androgynous beauty. She blinked twice and stared at me, as if I were a puzzle she couldn't quite resolve.

"The beach," I murmured.

She exhaled loudly and I squeezed her hand, too hard.

With renewed purpose, she turned and pulled me gently toward the sea.

We didn't speak as we moved through the darkness, but our entwined fingers danced, exploring each other's hands and wrists.

I stole a glance at her face. Her forehead was creased with anxiety and I wondered if she were afraid or troubled. We were moving quickly, but I didn't want to wait.

I stopped suddenly. The cobbled road to the beach was deserted and in the relative silence I thought for a moment I could hear my own heart beat. "Is this okay?" I asked nervously.

She sidled close to me and I felt her warm breath on my cheek as she whispered in my ear. "I like the beach."

With her so intimately close, the raw energy was overwhelming; I wanted her so much that I ached and I felt the excitement building inside me, like an untamed animal, slowly rousing from its sleep.

Her scent was intoxicating and I breathed in deeply; a heady mix of fragrances: mango, citrus, spice and the unique smell of her body. I closed my eyes and kissed the damp skin of her neck, causing her to gasp. She pulled me tightly against her and my stomach tumbled violently. "Let's go to the beach," she whispered.

I walked in a daze, only vaguely aware where we were going, as she led me from the road and through the tamarisk trees lining the beach. She stopped in a clearing, her eyes twinkling in the ethereal light. "Here?" she asked, her breath coming in short, sharp gasps. I shook my head. "By the water," I said and guided her further into the darkness.

Finally reaching the shore, I stopped. The ocean lapped rhythmically against a swollen mound, fashioned by its relentless, tidal advance. I turned to face her, suddenly afraid. The feelings she evoked were distantly familiar and confronted by them, I felt awed and tiny. Apparently sensing my trepidation, she moved closer. "Are you alright?" she asked, moving closer.

"Yes."

She tilted her head to one side, studying me curiously. "Have we met before?" she asked.

"I... I don't know... I feel that I know you."

She rested her hand on my waist, her touch light and electrifying. I started involuntarily at the contact and she smiled. "What do you want?" she asked.

I hesitated and looked into her eyes. "I want… you."

Then she kissed me and everything stopped.

We were fixed in an instant, beyond everything that is and was and ever would be; as though we had no right to have ever been anywhere but joined in that moment together.

Suddenly I was overcome with a passion I hadn't known before. It started in my core and radiated outward until there was nothing beyond the feeling; a deep, terrible longing that seemed as if it might consume me and in an instant, we were prostrate together on the cool sand, struggling free from our clothes.

And then she was on top of me, her naked flesh warm and smooth against my own.

I felt the firm skin of her nipples and as she brushed against my thigh, the hot fluid of her arousal trailed over my skin.

Her mouth fixed firmly on mine, her tongue probing and searching. I moaned as she sucked my lips and teased me, flicking her tongue and biting gently.

I dug my fingernails into her back and pulled her hard against me, willing her to satisfy the hunger.

She ground her hips, urging herself against my centre and I felt the heat from her and gasped as my stomach contracted violently.

Sliding her hands around my back, she moved against me slowly at first, then worked up to a smooth rhythm. I sighed as we connected and a bolt like electricity trembled inside me. She writhed on top of me, kissing my neck and breasts hungrily.

I felt the surge grow in my core and I arched fiercely against her. She knew I was close and moved away.

"Not yet," she said kissing my throat, my shoulders then moving down to my breasts.

Anticipation welled inside me as she took my nipples in her mouth, sucking gently and then massaging each in turn with her tongue. I groaned and ran my fingers through her hair, longing for her to fulfil the promise.

With agonizing care she moved down my stomach, kissing me slowly and tracing every inch of flesh with an expert tongue. Her hands glided over my body, down my legs, then back and forth inside my thighs.

I could think of nothing except her inside me, and my pulse roared in my ears as I willed her onward. I felt the heat of her mouth as she brushed my groin with her lips and moved inevitably down.

As she finally fixed her mouth over me, I grabbed her head with both hands. Her tongue slid down and entered my forcefully. The sensation was blissful and I arched back in ecstasy. She rocked my hips against her mouth, pushing further and harder with her tongue. I wrapped my legs around her neck and ground against her. I could sense her growing excitement and she moaned and held me tightly.

She began to work her tongue over my swollen centre and she covered me with her mouth, releasing wave after wave of excruciating pleasure.

I heard singing somewhere in the distance; a plaintive lament of lost love, and for a few sweet moments, I was displaced; immersed somewhere in the dark territory of my mind, where there were only the sad strains of the song, and the sensation, building and building until I could barely stand it.

In one swift movement she slid her fingers deeply inside me.

And that was as much as I could bear.

The climax ripped through me and I cried out, rolling backwards and squeezing her against me with unintentional force.

I was lost, my mind black, consumed entirely by the wonderful sensation of her love.

Tides of bliss swept over me as she reached inside me, deeper and deeper until I could take no more. Finally exhausted, I fell back, my body spent.

She withdrew gently and knelt across me, watching in silence as I lay motionless, and gasping for breath.

Tenderly, she took me in her arms and held me against her, whispering soothing words in my ear. I don't remember now what she said exactly, but I do recall feeling euphoria at that moment, which seemed both familiar and strange in equal measure.

She lay down beside me on the sand, stroking my hair and I opened my eyes to stare up at the immense, night sky. A billion stars blinked down at me from behind a clement moon. Beside us the ocean continued its relentless dance against the shore and the sound of their tenuous embrace was almost musical.

I turned to face her and she smiled. The moonlight accentuated her beauty and I kissed her. Stroking her face gently, I sighed. "I want to make love to you."

She returned my kiss and pulled away. "There's no need. I am completely satisfied."

She watched me for some time then, until finally she stood and dressed quickly, so I did the same.

Taking me by the hand, she led me across the beach, through the tamarisk trees and to the dark, cobbled streets beyond. In silence we moved back to the bright lights of the town and in no time at all, were dodging tourists on the busy streets beside the promenade. We returned to the bar where we had met earlier that evening and I sat in the same chair. She stood before me and smiled a quizzical smile; her gaze penetrating.

Moonlight stole through the broken canopy overhead as it shifted in the wind and pale light danced momentarily across her face.

Before I could stop myself, I spoke. "Will I see you again?" and immediately I regretted the words. For a moment neither of us spoke. She held out a hand to me and I reached out, caressing her fingers with my own.

She was suddenly serious. "There is a poem I know.

'Has this been thus before?

And shall not thus time's eddying flight

Still with our lives our love restore?'

it." I was puzzled, but nodded my agreement. "Yes… I know of

She sighed, smiled and then she was gone.

Summer of Samantha

Melody Breyer-Grell

Melody Breyer-Grell has been active in the creative arts since childhood. This classically trained opera singer turned to jazz and has put out an award-winning debut CD - *The Right Time.* Melody chronicled the ups and downs of pursuing music in the hysterical "What's Funny about Jazz? - A Show for Nobody"

Grell's song lyrics helped her secure and become a senior contributor (interviews, features and reviews) for *Cabaret Scenes Magazine*. Melody is a prolific contributor to "The Huffington Post" and is making her fiction debut in SunKissed.

HOW MAURA ENDED UP in Manhattan during the scorching summer of 1977 is a mere coincidence, but times were hot all around. The long-running, murderous nightmare - *Son Of*

Sam (David Berkowitz - he had already killed or injured over ten people) was being played out and NYC was yet to experience the peak of the dark drama in its extreme midsummer madness that was the Great Blackout of '77.

Maura, a rather vocally prodigious operatic soprano at 19 years of age had a personality not unusual to young singers - a bit needy - yet very vivacious with a balance of over-confidence and insecurity. Although she was a beauty in her own way, her body, more Botticelli than Twiggy, kept her permanently self-conscious in a time when "thin was in." Long, chestnut hair, malleable blue eyes and sculpted cheekbones completed the picture of a girl whom although not yet 20 had had a series of brief, confusing sexual encounters (not uncommon during the disco era) yet still felt in need of a boyfriend most desperately. Maura was stilted and fearful around the opposite sex - often overcompensating with flirtations bravado. Put off by the "good boys", she had not allowed herself to experience positive male companionship.

Julliard's summer music students, Maura among them, were housed in a section of the historic Hotel Ansonia, a relic of the past, including the tenancy of Enrico Caruso, Babe Ruth, and Igor Stravinsky.

Returning back to the hotel around 8:00 PM, having been tutored for her upcoming and arduous counterpoint (no subject a singer needed!) exam, she bumped into, and was invited to the apartment of her neighbor, Samantha, a graduate piano student whom Maura had not noticed much, as it was rare for them to pass each at school or the Ansonia.

Samantha was Maura's symmetrical opposite. Almond eyed and olive skinned, she was an unusual product of a multi-cultural (was that politically correct expression even used in the 70's?) marriage of a Samoan father and British, Jewish mother. She was born in Leeds and after finishing her undergrad at the renowned local conservatory, was taking her graduate degree at Julliard. Her apartment was filled with exotica (dark spirited masks from her father's side and Judaica from her mother) - possessing a sense of mysticism as opposed to the diet-cola can littered "flop" of the American Jewish girl from Long Island.

"Would you like a spot of tea"...Samantha inquired in a British accent that was jarring - due to her decidedly non British appearance.

"Oh yes and 'ow about a loverly scone" Maura mimicked her new friend and laughed. She always became a bit sarcastic with strangers, a habit she picked up from her gay male friends to control her nerves and break the ice.

Samantha grinned indulgently and with an exaggerated cockney accent, joked back offering up some non-existent "crisps and pop."

"Actually I gotta go pretty soon, gotta sing early for Eleanora

Stanly's vocal master class tomorrow morning."

With a naughty laugh, Sam admitted she was not only cognizant of the class, but had just found out she was the scheduled accompanist. Sam, a fledgling concert pianist, had to do such things to complete her graduate degree.

"G' night then, look forward to playing with, I mean for you" cooed Sam playfully, as she gently but surprisingly hugged Maura and pecked her cheek, who upon exiting almost skipped down the hallway.

***

"Hey, I just met a really fun girl down the hall" Maura announced , taking a swig out of a flat, warm bottle of Diet Pepsi as she plopped down on the lumpy, formerly gold velveteen couch, slamming the soda on the cheap wooden coffee table that fronted it.

Christie, Maura's roommate, was another Long Island girl, of similar background, but Irish rather than Jewish; tall, skinny with long frizzy red hair and a face full of freckles. A bit homely, but very confident and alluring in her own way, she was hooked up for life. Her steady boyfriend John was an affair that was consummated at their drunken senior cast party. Maura, who envied this woman's complete comfort around men, was glad to find her home that night, relaxing with a copy of Cosmo, smoking a Marlboro Light and knocking down a brew. A talented violist, she was also in the summer, all scholarship programme.

"You don't mean that girl Samantha, do you? You know what she is, don't you?" At that time even the nicest people could be very closed-minded.

"What? No, wait. Hmmm..." Maura trailed off.

"You know what I mean." Christie was rolling her eyes - "Gay, a lesbian, likes women. You don't need that in your life. Be careful." Christie also knew Maura was prone to depression and things never rolled off her back lightly.

"Well, I don't really know about that, and so what if she is? It hardly will put me in *danger*. I am as *straight* as they come."

And Maura did believe she was straight, although sometimes she *was* stimulated when it came to the exposure of two women acting out erotically - but she did not really process it as important information. Just last week, (in downtown's Greenwich Village) she had seen Bernardo Bertolucci's WWll era epic and "art film," *The Conformist*. The movie had a scene where two beautiful Italian women of opposite appearance (one blonde, one brunette), had taken to the floor of a romantic, lantern lit Italian dance hall. It was a magical scene and Maura found herself squirming in her movie seat. But she never acknowledged it as prescient to her.

"Well, just watch out. She probably has her eye on you, and you know that is not what you really want."

***

Maura was almost defeated by her pantyhose, struggling to dress herself that morning. As she entered Julliard - fearing that her face of make-up was melting, she bounded into the bathroom for a freshen up and spotted a cool and crisp Samantha, washing her surprisingly delicate (at least for a pianist's) hands.

Samantha was really starting to hold a fascination for Maura. Gay or not, the singer thought that Sam was just about perfection. Naturally slim, yet inoffensively muscular, she wore a gray, simple silk blouse with a ruffle down the center and stylish bolero pants, which cinched her waist. No make-up was needed and the only jewelry she displayed was a simple gold chain necklace and a rather expensive, delicate gold watch. Her short nails were carefully manicured with clear polish and her thick, almost kinky hair was pinned in a loose bun.

"We are early - let's take a look at your music," Sam lightly offered.

Maura, who could be insecure about just anything, was sure about one thing - she had the voice and she knew how to use it. Samantha was not surprised by the ornately florid piece thrown in front of her and easily played the intro as Maura's voice rang out true and strong, yet flexible possessing a natural lyric sound of velvet.

"Well, that was nice," Sam commented without inflection (Maura was kinda annoyed that she did not rave.) "Let's go. I saw the list. You are second up."

Maura heard her name being called and approached the stage with confidence and a bit of swagger - she had been singing "Juliet's Waltz" since she was 16 and was not worried about pulling if off. And it looked like her new friend Sam was more than a competent accompanist, so even if it were not her chosen gig, she was a pro.

But nothing in music or baseball performance is a sure thing, no matter how good you look in the bull-pen.

The trouble started when Maura handed her music to Sam. The pianist had a brief question that required the singer to bend her head over toward her, and just by brushing by her hair by a wisp Maura felt her knees go weak, not a good start for a "diva" getting ready to begin her rondo.

Adrenalin pumped through her veins and she moved far away from Sam, let out a big exhale, set her feet firmly on the ground (ala Maria von Trapp) and managed to get through the aria skillfully, although a bit mechanically, which did not go unnoticed by the great diva, Stanly.

"Miss Stein -- Nice singing, lovely voice, but that is not enough to make a great career on. Do you know why?"

"Uh..."

The diva went on - not waiting for a reply. "The whole point, your singing, however beautiful or technically secure - might get you steady work but it won't move an audience to personally identify with you - you must express the emotion of what your character is feeling. Each word should convey the meaning attached to it. Your vocals were on the money but the lyrical phrases lacked, well, lyricism!

Maura, never having been so fully scrutinized, sneakily exited the school, ran back to the Ansonia, tore off her pantyhose, and ripped them into shreds screaming to Christi, "Fuck me, you are right, I should have watched out for that witch - she messed me up, I never want to see her again. Fuck her! I hate her. She can take her perfect dyke ass and go blow herself up! I am going to rest."

Often, going "to rest" meant locking the bedroom door, accompanied by a pint of Haagan-Dazs, the new ice cream sensation that was to cause many people even more difficulty with their "diets."

But Maura was not to be comforted and fell into a deep snooze letting the ice cream melt in the carton next to her little twin bed, located near the window facing the outside brick wall, next to their small bedroom.

Always a vivid dreamer, she had flashes of the master class, the girl down the hall, her parents' angry disappointment and the fear of becoming a has-been before she was 20.

***

On the weekend of the 17th, Christi went to Boston to visit John (he wisely avoided music, being an engineering student at MIT) leaving Maura alone to contemplate the heat and her loneliness. What to do? Practice, practice. Feeling her body open up and her mind expand - singing rarely ceased to take Maura out of herself - she was trying to put the class in its proper perspective and pushed on mentally, as she had done since childhood.

She was at the climax of the passionate "Un Bel Di" when she heard a knocking on her door. It was Sam. Maura attempted to give the pianist a casual hello, but the wobbly feeling returned to her knees and she was speechless.

"Can I come in?"

"Sure, Ok." Maura did not really know how or even why to say no at this point.

As always, cool as a cucumber, Samantha looked especially comfortable in her tapered jean shorts and soccer shirt.

"Maura, I don't get it. What is with the cold shoulder since the master class? I thought we were becoming friends. I love your voice and..."

"I have never been as embarrassed as I was last week, if you did not notice. I don't know what happened but it can't happen again. This scholarship..."

"I know this scholarship is all we all have! I would never be accompanying unless I needed to get the credit... for my professorship. That does not mean I don't appreciate..."

"So you don't care at all about us singers?" Maura was again breathless and did not know why.

"Bollocks! Do you have any idea how spoiled you sound? You did very well - a master class format is created for teachers to share comments; if not, who would learn anything? Don't you get it?"

Maura was doubly embarrassed when she realized the truth in her neighbour's words. Sam finally was showing a bit of crack in her facade, as Maura noticed there was a tiny bit of sweat on her upper lip. She moved in to flick it off her and Samantha suddenly planted a firm, probing kiss on Maura's pink lips.

"Stop it! I was warned about you. Don't you know I am straight? Please leave. I don't want this," she cried, flushed and confused, ignoring what her body was saying to her, as a tingling traveled downward from back of her neck to her groin reigniting the sensation she had experienced at the movies.

Sam stepped back and sadly said, "Thou protest too much" - as she made her way back to her "flat" as she called it, leaving the door ajar, the effect being even more distressing for the cowed and dithered girl.

Maura was always able to compartmentalize, and this incident was not something she chose to reflect on. It seemed that Sam was finished with her anyway. When the women passed in the hall they did not acknowledge each other, although sometimes Maura would hear the strains of Liszt and Rachmaninoff being practiced repetitively and meticulously - usually ending the day with a stunningly passionate play off of her work.

***

Most folks of any means were out of town that weekend - it was just too hot. Maura had no desire to return to her overly curious parents and with Christi gone she had that special type of mid-summer loneliness, the nature of which one feels as if the only person abandoned on an alien planet, with no hope of rescue. Harboring those gloomy thoughts, she ventured out to the corner deli, purchasing some fruit, turkey roll (diet again) and some sugar-free Velamints. While checking out she noticed a split second blinking of the lights and thought nothing of it.

Exiting the elevator she again noticed the blinking, but also something quite more distressing. Maura had neglected to take her keys with her. And then it happened - the lights went out and the great black out of '77 commenced, with one lone girl adrift in a city covered by a steaming dark black blanket of emptiness.

No elevator service, no keys, roommate away. There was only one choice and that happened to be an exotic little piano player, the only person she ever got to know - even slightly, on her floor.

She took a breath and tapped on the door.

"I am sorry to bother you."

"What can I do for you? Do you need a candle? I might have another one" - without inviting her in.

"Sam, look, this is very embarrassing, but I don't have my key and there are no lights and SAM can I stay with you?"

There was no glint in her eye as Sam flatly agreed to her request.

"I was getting ready to go to sleep" she said formally - "here is a tee shirt for you," handing Maura an oversized crew top.

Samantha turned her back on Maura and moved all the way to the far side of the bed and Maura gingerly stepped inside.

The window was open and there was a miraculous breeze billowing through a very sheer oriental drape. Though it was the city, Maura could swear there was the fragrance of honeysuckle permeating the musky room.

Although the girl on the opposite side of the bed gave no indication that Maura existed, the singer could no longer fight what her body craved as she whispered,

"If you want to try what you did before..."

Even before Maura even finished her sentence Samantha turned around and gently kissed Maura's lips. Maura inhaled Sam's breath, at first as if it were a delicacy, taking in more and more carbon in as Sam's kisses became less gentle and more demanding, rubbing her hand across Maura's erect nipples, only to start sucking on them and nibbling on them like a puppy's gentle mouthing.

"Oh God, um oh Sam, um" she cried as her new lover touched her in a way that she had never been touched before, tickling her so predictably, yet randomly as to cause the wracking of Maura's whole body into an inevitable climax, as she had only previously felt when partaking of the music of Wagner and Puccini; these sensations being deeply internal contrasting the external passion aroused by great romantic music.

"Sam, why me?" Maura queried, after handling Sam in a way so private that she could not have imagined such a thing existed 24 hours ago.

"Silly, I heard you singing in the hall for 6 weeks and after the first time I saw you I knew I had to have your silly straight ass. Plus you have great boobs."

"My singing?"

"Well it ain't your overbite, although that is pretty cute. Don't you understand? We can both make us better than we already are! When you thought you crashed and burned at the Master Class, it was clearly an opportunity for a breakthrough. You can sing your ass off, but as Madame Stanly says, that is not the point. Listen to Callas. Her voice, not considered - though I do - beautiful, but her singing was so exciting that men got into poof fist-fights over her! I want to help you. You can help me. I love you, you idiot!

"Well... does that mean I am a lesbian then?" Maura mused, dreamily.

"I won't swear for you, but I know I am, and we will make beautiful music together. Isn't it that what it is all about for both of us?"

As if on cue, the electricity was restored, and they realized that they had not left the bed for 24 hours.

Maura, her gait slightly weaving as she left the bed, wandered towards Sam's kitchenette and without even asking her hostess, started scavenging for food, only finding some warm yogurt.

"Feeling peckish, are you?"

"Ha, I have pecked enough, I am ravenous."

"Well, who cares! Let's start practicing!!!"

"Practicing what my dear? I think we have found perfection."

"I can see now what needs to be done when your Juliet is at the balcony. If I played softer, so you can pick up some... some small..."

"Well, maybe after you go out and get me some ice cream. I *am* a diva you know – I'm *your* diva..."

Retreat
Niamh Murphy

SHE THEW HER CASES on the bed and with that swift movement she felt as though she'd had something removed.

The weight of her stress was cast off and she threw back her arms and head, stretching and yawning, as the relief of solitude rushed through her.

'Alone at last!' She thought.

Then her phone rang. She sighed in resignation and grabbed it from her handbag.

"Grace." She said firmly, needing no other greeting.

"Oh! Miss... erm... er... Grace, I'm glad I caught you!"

It was her pointless new PA. She'd thought that a personal assistant was supposed to *'assist'* her, not faff about like an inebriated chicken. But Pippa McLearny had so far proven her wrong on that count.

"Yes Pippa?" She said, not bothering to mask her irritation.

"It's the plastics order for the 'Grays' presentation…"

"What about it?"

"They've just called to say they won't be able to deliver and the presentation is tomorrow…"

Grace breathed deeply, feeling the stress rising again.

"Right" she said forcing herself back into business mode "plastics… what plastics exactly?

"For the presentation."

"Do you mean acetate?"

"Erm…"

Grace heard keyboard tapping, Pippa was clearly oblivious to exactly what it was she was asking for help with.

"Yes! That's right it's acetate for the presentation tomorrow; 'creative' want to print out a number of their designs onto acetates to provide a more tangible experience to the client."

Grace sighed, exasperated. She had always worried that a team of creative people were unable to come up with a more creative name than 'creative' for their department.

"You'll just have to go out and buy some acetate." She said wearily.

"But that'll affect the costings!"

"Look, is there any way you can get the acetate delivered in time for the presentation?"

"No…"

"Do you *have* to have the acetate for the presentation?"

"Yes—"

"Then you will have to go out and *buy* acetate, even if it is four times the price."

"But—"

"NO!" Grace was sharper than she'd intended. "I don't want to hear it Pippa. That's it. I'm switching my phone off."

She didn't listen to the protests. She held down the 'off' button and watched the touch-screen disappear, then threw it on the bed with the rest of her detritus.

"No more." She said.

She wandered over to the French windows, where long muslin drapes hid the view. Pulling them back, she drank in her surroundings.

The health retreat was in a huge acreage of countryside and from here she could see for miles. There was not a town, an office or even another building in sight. Just trees and grass and gardens and there, just beyond the cliff's edge, she could see the sparkling blue line of sea, twinkling in the heavy sunlight.

Grace rested against the door-frame and closed her eyes, listening.

Nothing.

No traffic, no phones, no sirens, no shouting, no typing, no questions, no people. Just peace. And just below the silence, in a place she could never normally hear, there were the birds and even at this distance she could hear the waves crashing against the rocks at the high tide.

'*Just me*' she thought. '*No one else. No one else is coming near me or speaking to me for a week.*'

Grace wandered down to the restaurant. She'd started getting restless in her room and wanted to try out some of the menu she'd seen online. But as the stepped into the lobby, she noticed the restaurant was closed. She looked at her watch; four thirty.

'Surely they should be open?' She thought.

She considered waiting in the bar but even for her it was a bit early. Besides she had chosen this hotel for its grounds and solitude, so she ought to make use of them.

She turned and walked across the tiled lobby and out of the grand entrance into the gardens.

There was a warm haze on the air and although the sun was starting to cool, heat from the long summer's day was yet to fade, even with the soft breeze coming off the ocean.

She took a right and slowly headed along the path round the side of the hotel. There was no rush; she could afford to drift along the gravel path, run her hand through the tall plants running along the side of the hotel and stop to stare at a small fountain in the middle of a courtyard.

As she made her way towards the back of the hotel she saw that the gardens opened up to a huge lawn with a few scattered trees. She could see tennis courts on the far side and to the left, near a little copse of wood, was a walled garden.

Intrigued, Grace headed towards it.

A long fish-pond, strewn with lilies, ran down the middle surrounded by a flagstone path and perfect hedgerows. Statues of classical figures peeped out of the undergrowth, as if they had been there since the fall of Troy. On the far side of the walled garden was a small mock-Grecian temple with a stone bench, perfectly placed to capture the afternoon sun.

Grace wandered over to it and sat down. She closed her eyes and basked in the warmth of the sun, listening to the distant waves and the occasional cooing of a wood pigeon.

She heard footsteps and opened her eyes momentarily, catching a glimpse of a woman in a long white dress, walking towards her. She was slow and graceful, her dress hugged her curves and for a moment Grace allowed herself to imagine that one of the statues of a Greek goddess had come to life. She closed her eyes again, dismissing the thought and enjoying the sun.

The footsteps slowly drew closer. But Grace determinedly ignored them trying to absorb herself in solitude and retreat from the world.

"Beautiful isn't it?"

Her inner self was screaming *'Me! Me! Me!'* But she forced her eyes open, searching for the owner of the voice.

The woman was just a few feet away, her face was angled towards the sun with a soft smile on her lips, the sunlight gave her an ethereal glow and sparkled on her auburn hair.

"Beautiful." Replied Grace.

She tore her gaze away, forcing herself not to stare and leaned back once more, closing her eyes.

The woman slowly drifted away without another word.

Grace couldn't help but open an eye to watch her leave, before silently admonishing herself.

'Strictly no flirting.'

The salmon had been exquisite and the gateaux divine, even with the raspberry coulee. She looked at the clock; it was six forty five and still bright outside.

She'd brought a book and there was a television in her room as well as a huge bath, so she *could* spend the evening relaxing and then get an early night, but she had a restless energy that needed to be purged.

Her mind kept drifting over work matters; all the stress that had built up over the last, manic, six months. She needed to cleanse her mind and to be away from people. But when she pushed those thoughts away, the image of the woman in garden replaced them; the way her body had moved as she walked down the path, the softness in her voice and the radiant glow of her skin.

Cleansing her mind was going to be difficult.

She decided to wander over to the bar and order a small red wine and finding a brochure, began leafing through it, occupying herself by planning out how she could work through every spa treatment the hotel could offer and maybe every cocktail as well.

The barman placed her drink in front of her and on a whim she asked if he had any ideas for how to spend the evening. He mentioned there was a wine-tasting class in the cellar. At first she thought it a little odd that there was a wine-tasting course in a health retreat, but decided it was exactly the kind of event that would take her mind off everything.

The cellar was dark and dusty: there were old lamps hanging from the walls and gothic arches leading off down different corridors, all lined with wine racks. In the centre of the room were two circular tables surrounded by high backed chairs, giving off more of an impression of a séance rather than a wine-tasting class.

Grace sat in the only place that still had a free chair on both sides but it didn't take long for someone to sit down next to her.

"Hello again."

She turned in surprise to see the woman from the gardens, smiling radiantly and she couldn't help but smile back.

"Hello!" She replied, convinced she must be blushing.

"I'm Alex." The woman said, holding out her hand.

Grace slid her hand into Alex's and her heart beat slightly faster as their skin touched.

"Grace." She said, quickly withdrawing her hand and determinedly looking across the room as their host began to talk. She hoped that she would be able to ignore her attraction to this woman and focus on distracting herself.

Grace thought she knew her wines, but she'd never really sat down and compared them. She liked the first very much, but she felt the second may have had more 'body' to it, the third was delightfully fragrant and by the fourth she'd learned the name of everyone on the table, had told the story of the time her brother lost a mattress on the A2 and had started flirting outrageously with Alex.

As the last of the wine was poured, people started to leave their seats and wander about the cellar, mingling with the other guests, complementing the course leader and purchasing their favourite wine of the night. But Grace and Alex remained at their table.

"You know, I think I may be more than a little drunk." Alex whispered.

Grace laughed.

"That could have something to do with the wine!"

Alex giggled before finishing off the rest of her drink.

"Shall we make a run for it before they persuade us to buy something?" She asked as she put down her empty glass. Grace looked at her, she knew she shouldn't, but she also felt that the offer of running away with Alex was too tempting to turn down.

They abandoned their table and sneaked past the other guests, running out into the abandoned lobby. Alex took hold of Grace's hand and led her up the main stairs onto the first floor, stopping outside one of the rooms and leaning against the wall.

"This is me." She said looking at Grace. "I've had fun this evening."

"Me too," whispered Grace, aware she was getting dangerously close to something complicated.

Suddenly Alex reached out and gently pulled Grace toward her and Grace didn't resist; allowing herself to be taken in Alex's arms. When Alex kissed her, she responded and before she knew what she was doing, her hands were running along Alex's waist and their bodies slowly bonded together.

A door slammed somewhere in the building, snapping Grace out of the moment.

She pulled away from Alex.

"I should go," she said, and, without looking back, she headed down the hall to her own room.

She wandered aimlessly around the gardens.

At least that's what she told herself.

She told herself that she was merely going for a morning stroll to clear her head after a late night. But she quickly found herself back in the walled garden with the Greek statues. She took her place on the bench remembering the events of the night before. She felt so stupid, like a teenage girl with a crush.

That morning she'd already walked around the hotel, looking in the restaurant and the pool, wondering if she should sign up for a spa treatment, just in case she might 'accidently' bump into Alex. Part of her was hoping that she would and yet another part was praying that she wouldn't. On the one hand she felt as though she had made a fool of herself the night before; leading Alex on and then running away.

Yet she knew she had done the right thing.

Her life was so hectic at the moment. She'd been running herself ragged, working painfully long hours and never taking a day off. She knew that if she didn't take time away to just stop and clear her mind that she would run herself into the ground. Then when she did take a week to recuperate, she spent the whole time fawning over a woman she had just met and worrying herself stupid over a fleeting, drunken kiss.

She wanted the world to just stop spinning so she could have a moment to catch her breath.

Eventually she decided there was no point in wandering around hoping to catch sight of someone that she didn't want to see. Instead she would go to the restaurant, order the next dish on her 'must-try' list and then spend the afternoon in the spa with her eyes closed and her face covered in avocado.

"May I join you?"

Grace looked up; it was Alex.

She was wearing a little black dress and her auburn hair framed her delicate face. She smiled at Grace and then raised an eyebrow, clearly waiting for a response.

"Yes! Yes of course." Stammered Grace, unsure if she was terrified or delighted.

"Did you miss me?" asked Alex cheekily, as she took her seat.

Grace managed to laugh.

"It has been quite dull," she admitted.

As they waited for their orders to arrive, Alex chattered about her morning. She'd been up the coast to a small fishing village for a look around and although Grace would have been exhausted by the expedition, Alex was clearly invigorated by it. Grace found herself energised by their conversation and the exuberance that seemed to ooze from Alex's very core. She was happy watching her talk, observing her movement and occasional flirtations, but there was still the nagging reluctance clawing at the back of her mind.

When dessert arrived, Alex was delighted by it and insisted that Grace try some of hers. She held the spoon out to her and Grace was helpless to resist. She leaned in closer and tasted the dark chocolate truffle.

"It's divine isn't it?" Alex whispered, and Grace couldn't deny that she agreed.

She found herself being led along by Alex and she wanted to take control back. She needed to be in charge and she needed to make this stop before it got out of control.

"I think" she said with firm tone, looking directly at Alex "I'm going to head upstairs after lunch and spend the afternoon in my room."

"Well" said Alex with one raised eyebrow, "I can't argue with that." Then suddenly she leaned closer "I think it's a marvellous idea."

Grace gasped as she felt Alex gently rest her hand on her thigh, the sudden, unexpected contact sending a rush of adrenaline through her. She knew then that she was losing control.

"In fact" whispered Alex, barely loud enough for Grace to hear "I think I might go up to my room now."

Alex stood and left the restaurant.

Grace was stunned for a moment and simply watched her leave. She couldn't quite believe that Alex had taken her suggestion that way and wasn't sure if she should be flattered or concerned. She didn't need the strain of dealing with this situation and wondered if she should follow Alex and explain or whether that would make her look more of a fool, but then not going would be just as bad.

She massaged her temples. She didn't want to have to deal with this anxiety; she had come here to get away from stress.

Reluctantly, she realised she would have to follow Alex. She needed to explain. She left her table and hurried across the lobby up the stairs, back to where they had kissed the night before. Alex was just unlocking her door. She looked up at Grace and smiled.

"Do you want to come in?" Alex's voice was low, just above a whisper and heavy with seduction. She held the door open slightly, looking at Grace, her little black dress clung to her body, begging to be ripped off. Grace forced herself to look away.

"Look, I'm not sure that this is such a good idea." Her body didn't agree, but she couldn't allow herself to be swallowed up by the moment.

"Must you always be the one in control?" Asked Alex, stepping closer. "Don't you ever just want to give up, run away from everything and let yourself go?"

Alex ran her fingers down the front of Grace's dress and looked straight into her eyes.

"I…"

"… to just stop thinking and worrying and to let someone else take the lead for a while."

"It's the middle of the afternoon…" Grace said, throwing out the only argument she had left.

Alex pushed open the door to her room and held out her hand. Grace felt that all her power to resist had been sapped away from her. Her ability to manage the situation and control others, had abandoned her and she found herself placing her hand in Alex's and being led into her room. And as she gave in and allowed herself to lose control, she finally realised that was exactly what she needed.

The Ballad of Iska and Marikit

Emma Rose Millar

DEEP IN THE SWIRLING MIST of Antique folklore lies a legend of two women; one young and beautiful by day but who by night assumes the terrible form of an evil, feathered demon who feeds on the blood of children through her long hollow tongue; the other, older and no-less attractive, who from the practices of the black arts has gained the power to sever her own head from her body and flies through the night with bat-like wings, with her bloody entrails sprawling behind her, preying on the foetuses of pregnant women. Her proboscis-like tongue can suck the very heart from an unborn child. This is the legend of vampires, the monstrous Aswang and Manananggal.

Antique, Philippines, November 1587

Iska lay naked on the banig, the sleeping mat she shared with Marikit. Her hair, black as the night sky, lay in silken strands strewn over her rough pillow of coconut matting, stuffed with the feathers of fairy-bluebirds and nightjars, and her breasts were uncovered. Marikit leaned over her and covered her with the sheet, kissing her protectively on the forehead. She stirred a little, "Are you going already Marikit?" she asked sleepily; the sun was only just rising.

"Yes," replied her lover, "I will not be long. Try to get some rest."

"I should come with you," murmured Iska, "I am a terrible burden Marikit; you are not my mother." She rolled over sleepily and showed Marikit the soft curve of her back.

Marikit left the hut, a tiny dwelling constructed from bamboo raised on stilts and sheltered by a thatch of anahaw leaves, bound for the rice fields of Antique.

"Marikit!" it was Datu, he made her jump.

"Oh goodness Datu! I did not see you there. You should not sneak up on me so. You look tired Datu." Although their fathers were cousins and they had grown up together there was something about Datu that Marikit did not like; he was always there somehow at her every turn. He unnerved her with his tendency to stand too close, to stare intensely, and to lay his hand too often on hers, or on her knee as they spoke. He was small with ferret like features and his fingernails were stained with tobacco.

"On your own again I see Marikit?"

"Yes, Iska had another seizure last night. She is sleeping it off. She seems to have more and more of them of late; I worry Datu, that she might die whilst I am gone, but the rice won't pick itself. We need to live on something."

Datu nodded knowingly. He had seen them last night, stood shrouded in the darkening shadows, peeping in through the window of their candle-lit hut, seen Marikit's firm buttocks rise up from the sleeping mat while she tucked her knees under her breasts and her hair flowed out over Iska's thighs. Iska lay squirming with a look of sheer ecstasy on her face, with her back arched and her eyes half-shut. He had stood so close he could almost taste them and heard their every sigh, their every gasp and then, as it was all over and they lay kissing and stroking one another's hair, Iska fell into a violent seizure and Marikit could do nothing but hold her until she collapsed sleeping in her arms like a baby. She had sung her a gentle lullaby which melted away on the breeze, "Matulog ka na, bunso, Ang ina mo ay malayo, at hindi ka masundo - Sleep now, youngest one, Your mother is far away, and she can't come for you."

Marikit continued on her way through the forest and the dappled light of the rising sun, but she did not seem to be able to shake Datu from her heels, "I am to be baptised this Sunday; I would be so happy if you could make it." He toyed with a copper crucifix, which he kept on a piece of string around his neck.

Marikit shifted uncomfortably, "I don't think so Datu, as I said I cannot leave Iska for too long.

"Then bring Iska with you."

"I am sorry Datu; we are of the old faith, as were you once. We do not hold with the Spanish way and I doubt very much that they would approve of our... of our lifestyle. Leave the Spaniards to their filthy inquisition and leave Iska and I in peace."

"But it is not right Marikit, the way you live; it is not what God wants! And it is bad for the village as a whole. If you do not follow his decrees then *The Lord will bring a nation against you from far away, from the ends of the earth, like an eagle swooping down, a nation whose language you will not understand, a fierce looking nation without respect for the old or pity for the young. They will devour the young of your livestock and the crops of your land until you are destroyed. They will leave you no grain, no wine or oil, nor any calves of your herds or lambs of your flocks until you are ruined.*"

"I thought the Spanish had already done that Datu; I shall rely on

Venus to protect our cultivated lands. My gods do not throw curses upon me; I worship only the morning star and the messenger Dian Masalanta who brought Iska to me on the rolling tide. Datu, Nimfa will be with you at your baptism, she is your wife; you do not need the likes of Iska and I there. And Datu, if you continue to follow me around I will have no choice but to speak to her. I don't want to, she has been my friend all of my life; do not force my hand in this Datu!"

"Do not go to Nimfa!" Datu grabbed hold of her arm.

"What are you doing Datu? You are hurting me."

"She is pregnant again; she is not to be upset. This may well be the last chance we ever get of having a child Marikit; we are none of us getting any younger. I beg you not to speak to her; you know how jealous she is of you."

"Then she should not be!" protested Marikit, "The two of you are wealthier than I, owing to you both having sufficient health for hard work. You keep more goats and chickens than me, you have a child on the way, and that is something I will never have; I have given up that chance to live with Iska, but I would not change it for the world; it is but a tiny price to pay." She wrenched her arm from his grip and continued down the mountain-side, whose summits were still shrouded in the morning's mist, and all the while he watched the sway of her slender back and the swishing of her beautiful hair, which hung in ripples around her waist.

Marikit continued to the fields, stacked up on terraces carved out of the green mountainside through which fresh-water streams and springs had been channeled, breathing life into the lush plants which poked out of the flooded ground beneath. She stooped, quickly plucking the greenery from the soil, tossing it into her fibrous woven basket, which she balanced on her hip and encircled with her supple arm. Over the previous months she had been employed planting the seeds in the nurseries and then transporting the tiny plants to the terraces; this was the final leg of the growing season after which the soil would be turned and rested ready for the next crop. Now she stood ankle-deep in the shallow floods, mingling with water buffalo and the other pickers of the wetlands and would spend the ensuing few months down in the mills.

Suddenly the silhouette of a woman slid across the yellow sun, "Oh Nimfa! I didn't see you there, how are you? Datu tells me you are with child again; you must be so pleased."

Nimfa nodded sadly, "I am Marikit. I think it is almost six months now; I have never carried this far before, but it is Datu, he seems to be getting worse. He is losing his sight, a film grows on the surface of his eyes and he says it is like looking through a fog. At night now he uses a stick and I can see him looking through the darkness as if a blizzard rages in front of his face. I worry that he will no longer be able to work and we will starve."

"I am sorry for your troubles Nimfa," said Marikit and she hugged her with all the compassion of an old friend.

Marikit worked late into the evening until the sun sank low behind the mountains and the sky was bathed in a pinkish sheen. "I have cooked you some food," said Iska, gladdened to see that her lover had returned. "You look weary Marikit. Here, sit down while I rub your back."

"Thank you," replied Marikit. "I am not so young as you." She looked around the hut; Iska had swept and strewn fresh herbs and there was milkfish and rice on the fire. "You are good to me," she smiled.

"I am sorry not to have been able to help you today Marikit." The last slivers of sunlight suddenly melted away and the sky went black. Violet clouds drifted slowly across the shining circle of the moon and the air was filled with the hollow calling of the night owl.

"That's alright; I picked enough for both of us in the end, nearly twice as much as Nimfa."

"Only when I woke this afternoon," continued Iska, "I thought to clean the hut, and when I did, I found this! I found it on our sleeping mat." She thrust the little copper crucifix accusingly into Marikit's hand.

"It belongs to Datu!" gasped Marikit. She could hardly bear to hold the little cross, but somehow could not release it from her grip. The copper seemed to burn into her hand and she squeezed it so hard that blood ran through her fingers and fell like the pitter-patter of rain to the floor. The silhouette of an eagle passed over the moon, "He has been here Iska, while you were sleeping. Datu has been here!"

"There is nothing else to be done," said Marikit angrily, "I will have to speak to Nimfa about this tomorrow; he has left me no choice."

They heard short breaths outside their window and the crackle of bracken underfoot; he had been there again; silently watching them from the shadows.

***

Datu ran blindly through the dense foliage, whose tones of emerald and jade had melted into the blackness of the night. It was true, he had been there that afternoon and had pulled back the sheet as Iska lay barely conscious, letting his failing eyes wander all over her breasts, her full thighs and her narrow calves. He had knelt down beside her, hovering above her with his breath upon her neck, wanting to touch her, wanting to touch himself. In the end he was suddenly horrified by what he had done and ran terrified into the forest, though he could not run from the disgust that consumed him.

Now he thought only of what Nimfa would do when she discovered his grubby secret; he crashed against tree trunks and stumbled across the ground-hugging species until breathless he rushed in through the door of his own hut, which he shared with Nimfa and her sisters Leizel and Tala.

"Whatever is the matter Datu?" Tala had been pounding a quantity of unhusked rice in a pestle and mortar. She was older than Nimfa as was Tala, and all three were weathered and had a sprinkling of grey hair to varying degrees. "You are white as a ghost; come and let us warm you."

"Oh Nimfa!" he cried pushing past her sisters as if they didn't exist, "I have seen something terrible! Dark forces are upon us

Nimfa and the whole village will be cursed. Crops will perish and we shall all be dead from famine."

Nimfa held Datu to her chest, tenderly stroking his hair, "What has troubled you so husband?"

"It is Marikit and Iska!" he clung to her smock with his yellowed fingers like a frightened child, "I have seen them, using their tongues on each other in all kinds of unnatural ways! Iska has a long and hollow tongue, pointed enough to pierce a man's skin, and Marikit has the tongue of a proboscis, like the snout of the long nosed monkey which can suck the heart from an unborn child. Then afterwards Iska falls to the floor in a convulsion Nimfa; she is possessed by the devil. I have seen them with my own eyes!"

"No Datu! You are mistaken."

"Nimfa," he whispered, "They sleep on pillows stuffed with their own feathers and screeching night-birds encircle their hut ready to lead them to their prey. You must not speak with Iska or Marikit. Do not go near them! I forbid it. They will snatch the child from your belly Nimfa; tell the children of the village they must sleep on the edges of their mats. They are among us… the aswang and the mannananggal are here!" He fell to the floor in a trance with his cloudy eyes rolling in his head.

***

"Good morning Leizel, Tala," cried Marikit, the two women stood in the wetlands beside their sister. "I have not seen you in an age!"

The ladies looked her way disdainfully and Marikit fancied she heard them hiss like wild cats. They turned away in disgust and huddled into a group, talking in hushed tones with each other.

"Oh hang them anyway!" laughed Iska, threading her arm through the crook of Marikit's elbow, "They do not understand our ways. They are jealous of our happiness!"

"It is easy for you," replied Marikit shortly, feeling the sharp stab of rejection, with tears springing to her eyes, "I have known these women since girlhood, they are my friends. I am sorry to snap at you Iska; Nimfa, Liezel, have I offended you in some way?" She extended her hand towards the three ladies but they shrank from her in abhorrence.

Iska bobbed her tongue out cheekily at the whispering ladies, to which Tala shrieked in horror, "Sweet Jesus Nimfa; she has licked our shadow!" and the three of them huddled together, their eyes wide with terror.

Marikit was crestfallen, suddenly feeling the lonely chill of an outcast in her own village, "There are strange things afoot Iska; I feel a terrible foreboding." A shiver went right through Marikit and the pair picked rice alone on the periphery of the terrace, away from the cluster of workers who toiled with the buffalo under the scorching sun. "Promise me Iska that if the Inquisition should ever take you, then you will confess to anything and accept the ways of their Lord."

"Never Marikit!" cried Iska, "I will not do it."

Marikit took her hands gently, "Ah, you are a proud woman Iska, but sometimes pride is not a strength. I ask you not to change what is in your soul; only you know what lies there. It cannot be stolen from you, just as Datu cannot steal my heart away when it will always lie with you. Promise me Iska."

The younger woman nodded solemnly, "If it pleases you Marikit."

***

Datu did not go to the terraces to pick rice that day; instead he made his way down to the Spanish church in the valleys, a construction of stone and coral labouriously crafted by indigenous and Chinese builders which was lavishly decorated with wall paintings and statues of ivory. A volute housing an ornate stairwell to the bell tower cast a spiralling shadow over its well-manicured grounds. Beside it lay a single storey monastery of stone, below which was a windowless dungeon, where water dripped down the walls, instruments of torture lay bloody and the air rang with the chilling screams of heretics

"Friar," whispered Datu, "I have come that I might speak with you."

Friar Xavier was engaged in solitary prayer dressed in a simple brown tunic and scapular with an ample hood and a wooden crucifix around his neck. He looked blankly at the intruder, slowly coming round from a period of quiet contemplation. "Yes Datu, I can see that you are troubled."

"Friar, it is the most terrible of matters," continued Datu in hushed tones, "There are heretics in the village, there is evil, there are those practicing paganism. The black arts are poisoning Antique, Friar."

"These are very serious allegations Datu," replied Xavier leaning forwards, "very serious indeed."

Datu nodded, "I do not come to you lightly, but the whole of our community is held fast in the clutches of danger. It is Iska and Marikit Friar; they live as husband and wife though they are both women. They beat drums and worship stars, they give talisman to each other as tokens of their love."

The Friar jerked backwards in shock. "You know what you are saying Datu? You are sure what you are saying is true? They will have to be handed over to the Inquisition, and may God have mercy on them."

Datu made the long ascent back up the mountainside, past the flooded terraces towards his own hut. He relied increasingly now on the familiarity of the rough terrain underneath his feet, so poor was his eyesight in the waning sun. Even as he emerged from the leafy forest into the shadowy glade he could hear a terrible wailing coming from his own hut. As he rushed up the creaking steps he saw Nimfa, lying on her sleeping mat, which was soaked in blood. She had clutched close to her chest something that at first glance seemed to be a tiny blue ball. He peered steadily through the gloam in front of his eyes until Tala cried out, "The baby Datu! She has lost the baby! This is the work of the aswang and the mannananggal; they have killed him while she slept! Come Datu, we know what we are to do."

The three of them stole through the darkening forest, through the hollow calling of bats and the quiet slithering of snakes, leaving the grieving mother where she lay. When they came across Marikit she was pounding some ginger to make salabat. She smiled warmly at Tala and Leizel in the belief that they had come to make amends for their earlier rudeness, "I am gladdened that you have come," she said, but they did not smile back. Even as they took hold of her arms she still believed they had come in friendship; it was only as they dragged her to the floor screaming like banshees and she saw Datu's looming shadow that fear finally crept over her and spread coldly through her bones. Then she felt a terrible crushing pain in her chest and heard the crunching of her ribs. Again and again the pain came in waves until finally it stopped.

When Iska returned from collecting firewood she was greeted by the soles of Marikit's feet sticking out through the doorway, she could hear the sad calling of the nightingale ringing around the glade. "Marikit?" she whispered cautiously. Iska stumbled backwards, dropping the armful of logs, which rolled away down the leafy slopes. They had driven a wooden stake right through her heart and scattered her lower torso with salt so that her body once segmented by her mannananggal self could not be re-joined and she would perish. The contortion of her face left Iska in no doubt of the horror that her lover had felt just at the moment of her death; the image of it would never leave her. "Oh Marikit!" she gasped, and then she turned and ran down the mountain side, tumbling and staggering as she fled, vultures circling around her with the taste of death in their beaks. She could not think, she could not breathe, it had not struck her even that Marikit was dead.

"Friar Xavier!" the hooded figure caught her in his arms, "Oh you must come quickly. There has been a murder, most monstrous. It is Marikit! We must help her."

"You are Iska of Antique?" he asked her calmly.

"Yes, they have done all kinds of sickening things; some kind of vile ritual has been forced upon her and…"

"Then you must come with me," he said gravely.

***

"Have you any idea why you are here?" Iska sat shaking in the dungeon with the prelates of the monastic orders bearing down on her.

"You cannot think I killed Marikit surely?" she asked in bewilderment.

"The Pope has decreed that anyone who attempts to construe a personal view of God which conflicts with Church dogma must be burned without pity." The faceless inquisitor loomed above her in his black robes, his head hidden in the dense folds of his hood, "you do admit that you are a pagan?" His stern voice resonated around the stone walls down which water ran in streams.

"Yes replied Iska," wide-eyed as a fawn, "I worship the morning star and the messenger who brought me love and granted fertility to our land."

"Then you must take accept the ways of the Holy Roman Church," he insisted, squeezing her hand until she felt a terrible crushing sensation in her fingers.

"I follow the old faith," she replied in all simple innocence.

"And you practice the black arts?" He leant forward and the edges of his hood brushed against her cheek; she felt his hot breath against her skin, "and together with Marikit of Antique you took the unborn child from your neighbour's belly and feasted on his blood?"

"No!" protested Iska, feeling a sickness rising in her guts. "If you knew Marikit, she was the most gentle, the most compassionate person. She would never, we would never! This is all a mistake!"

"It is no mistake!" raged the Inquisitor, "God does not make mistakes!" then he pressed his liver-coloured lips against her ear, "I exhort you to confess, Iska of Antique that your life may be spared; if you do not then both your life and your soul will be condemned for ever by God." He held a flagon of water to her trembling lips.

"I have nothing to confess!" cried the quivering girl. She thought of Marikit, of the way she died, the most torturous death. Screams from the sickening chambers echoed eerily along the labyrinth of twisting corridors, and she fancied she could hear Marikit screaming too. The bloodcurdling cries conjured horror not only from without, but from within Iska herself. Images depicting the worst kind of cruelty floated around her mind, of hot pokers being thrust into the orifices of heretics, of fingernails being slowly pulled from their cuticles and the hacking out of tongues with a blunt blade. Every time she tried to expel one picture from her brain another would be painted, more gruesome than the last.

"Perhaps then the strappado will persuade you." He beckoned in two hooded monks who were to scribble down her confession.

Iska was hauled up by a rope and was suspended from the ceiling with her back bent and her hands chained behind her back; heavy iron weights were shackled to her feet, then the rope suddenly went slack and she fell, being brought up sharply where upon every nerve of her body went into confusion and her arms were torn from their sockets. Again and again she was broken on the pulley and her screams seemed to erupt from her belly as if they came straight from the depths of hell, but still she maintained that there was nothing to confess.

"Her spells have rendered her insensible!" bellowed the Inquisitor, "She will die before she admits to it. Bring her down."

They stripped her and she cringed with the slow peeling of every layer until she stood completely bare with urine running down her legs. Humbled she stood while they eyed her, with not the means to cover her modesty until finally she stood up indignantly looking straight into the seemingly empty hood of her tormentor.

They lay her on the rack and stretched her, the lamp creaked on its hook, casting its gloomy light through the airless cell and she saw in horror the white stone walls smeared with blood and engraved with the inscription "*Glory be only to God*." They turned the wheels again and again until the Inquisitor finally shouted "Enough!" He drew back his hood and his face was as unremarkable as any Spaniard you might pass in the village, not really a monster at all. Beads of sweat glistened on his brow and he had a strange look of melancholy in his dark eyes, "You are a fool Iska of Antique. May God have mercy upon your soul."

Iska remained in the dark, chained all alone in the dungeons for two months, which may just as well have been two years, or twenty. She was starved and her hair shorn. Time meant nothing; she knew only that at intervals water was held up for her which she drank from greedily though it was never enough. Each time they came to her with water she could only wonder what kind of grisly act they might force upon her next; she spent every waking hour in a state of petrification and slept standing up, her nose filled with the stench of those who had died or taken their lives in the chambers of cruelty. In the end she was taken into the square outside the monastery of St. Francis with the brightness of the sun blinding her although the sky was quite overcast. Two guards supported her under her elbows and her feet dragged along the floor. The sickening smell of cooked meat permeated the air and she chocked back vomit, which burned her throat. With the jeering of the baying crowd ringing in her ears; she was strangled and tied to a stake where she was burned with a handful of other heretics whose children were flogged while they watched their parents die in agony. Even as the coals were lit she curled her toes away in panic, knowing deep inside that it was all over for her and there was no escaping the excruciation of what was to come. Nothing she had either experienced or imagined over the preceding months would prepare her for this; she had thought the end would be a release but now as the torch was held up to her she writhed helplessly to try and escape its heat. "She burns!" shrieked Nimfa as the glowing orange flames danced around her body. She had Datu supported by her elbow, his sight by now had completely failed him and the world was only a swirling mass of fog.

Through the flames Iska saw Marikit's face; she saw her arms unfolding, beckoning Iska towards her, she fell into her lover's arms and suddenly it was all over.

**

Datu and Nimfa made their way back up the mountainside, each carrying with them a terrible burden of disappointment. Nimfa herself had harboured such hatred for both Iska and Marikit and had wished upon them such atrocities but even as the flames had engulfed Iska there was a hollow feeling that the whole thing had been a terrible anti-climax. Her thirst for blood had in no way been sated and she climbed towards the summits knowing that the battle was finished, yet nothing had been won.

As they reached their hut a horrible sensation of emptiness crept over both of them. The sky was black and winds swirled through the forest, guyabano trees threw up their branches, tossing them wildly in the air like the arms of a thousand wailing women. Rain started to fall in sheets from the heavens, flowing back down the mountainside and spilling from the rice terraces like a great waterfall. The valley was engorged with water and the rain poured into the dungeons of the Inquisition but both the church and the monastery itself were spared.

Datu laid upon his sleeping mat and fell into a deep slumber. Through the depths of the mists emerged the face of Iska, yet changed; her hair was decorated with feathers which extended down her back into great wings. He saw the head of Marikit, severed, with her innards trailing behind her; they slid around his neck like a serpent and crushed him. He felt the sharp tongue pierce his chest and he started up right and in horror opened his eyes. For only a second the images of Iska and Marikit remained before him and then they began to fragment as if they were made from china; they disappeared into the darkness and the fog returned once more before Datu's eyes. In his panic, he had plunged his knife into his own chest; they had never really been there at all.

As the life drained from his body he heard a haunting melody which blew in on the tropical winds "Matulog ka na, bunso, Ang ina mo ay malayo, at hindi ka masundo - Sleep now, youngest one, Your mother is far away, and she can't come for you."

It was the ballad of Iska and Marikit flying freely through the forest of Antique.

**

REFERENCES

http://en.wikipedia.org/wiki/List_of_birds_of_the_Philippines

http://www.rnib.org.uk/eyehealth/eyeconditions/conditionsac/Pages/charles_bonnet.aspx

http://en.wikipedia.org/wiki/Nipa_hut

http://www.jewishvirtuallibrary.org/jsource/History/
Inquisition.html

http://www.thailandsworld.com/index.cfm

http://www.aboutnames.ch/phil.htm#Names

http://mananalaysay.blogspot.com/2010/07/social-life-in-16th-
century-philippines.html

http://www.vampiresvillage.com/tag/manananggal/

http://mananalaysay.blogspot.com/2010/10/16th-century-
paganism-in-philippine.html

More titles from Freya Publications

Strains from an Aeolian Harp

by **Emma Rose Millar**

1922: Charlie is a chancer, with a taste for gin, ragtime and women. Underneath his veneer of assurance however, is a man with a terrible burden of guilt. Fuelled by his fatal addiction to opium, Charlie's violent temper soon inflicts devastating consequences on the three women who love him, dragging each of them into a world they could never have imagined. In the face of his abject cruelty, one of them finds love in a place where she least expects it; the arms of another woman. Strains from an Aeolian Harp is the story of one woman's enduring strength and of a fragile bond between women in a society filled with prejudice and misogyny.

A Changing Girl by **Betty Flack**

A Changing Girl is the gripping portrait of Kate Moriarty, a young woman finding her way at a University still reeling from the recent disappearance of a student. Carrying her own secrets, Kate tries to fit in, but quickly finds herself drawn to Miriam, a friendless outsider, hell-bent on her own destruction. Intrigued by the missing girl and her connection with Miriam, Kate finds herself drawn into a dark and disturbing world where nothing is quite as it appears. A serious thriller, by a serious new writer. Betty Flack's A Changing Girl is a coming out story with a difference.

Loving Amélie by Sasha Faulks

Chris Skinner is struggling to recover from a lost love affair: an experience that has altered him. Previously happy enough to labour alongside his older brother Peter in their family restaurant, he briefly found new perspective on life and love in the form of the inimitable French beauty, Amélie Bénoit, who happened into his bistro one day and later into his bed.

Amélie is passionate and artistic, if fickle and flawed in her own appealing way. They shared a love of real food and great sex. Then she left him.

Entrusted with the care of their baby daughter, Amélie Christina, Chris embarks on a journey that takes him from London to Paris, via his childhood in the Midlands, to make sense of the ties that bind him: family unity, friendships and obsessive love.

Crossing the Line by Toni James

Rachel Ryder is training for the British Mountain Championships. After years of hard work, she's in the best shape of her life and a favourite to win the Championship. So the last thing she needs is a broken arm and a distracting encounter with a beautiful doctor. Matters become even more confusing when Rachel's treacherous ex-girlfriend arrives on the scene, determined to stop at nothing to win her back.

With the championships approaching and her heart in a storm, Rachel is forced to choose between the woman she lost, the woman she has found and her opportunity to realise the ambition of a lifetime.

The Lost Resort by Toni James

When Eve Harper finds her lover in the arms of another woman, she's forced to face up to some uncomfortable truths; she's single, the wrong side of forty and she's running out of wine!

There's nothing else for it, but to sell everything and take an extended holiday in Greece.

With her unruly younger sister in tow, Eve embarks on a tumultuous journey of self-discovery and en-route she meets Annie, a troubled teacher from England, Heidi, an ambitious hotelier and JJ, a cute bartender, with an uncanny gift for cocktails. When she arrives at *The Lost Resort*, a women-only hotel on the Greek Island of Lesbos, Eve finds her own slice of paradise and, with temperatures rising and passion in the air; she wonders where it will all end. But this is only the beginning. The Lost Resort is the first in a series of funny, romantic novels set on the Greek island of Lesbos. It is a story about friendship, family and the restorative power of love.

For more information or to purchase any of our titles please visit www.freyapublications.com or www.amazon.co.uk.

www.ingramcontent.com/pod-product-compliance
Lightning Source LLC
Chambersburg PA
CBHW061356280526
45784CB00001B/280